McCAUSLAND

December 6, 1979

Happy Birthday, Mom.

Hope you enjoy a numerous historical views of the city you know & I love!

Love,
Toni

Doc Maynard,
the Man Who Invented Seattle

DOC MAYNARD

The Man Who Invented Seattle

By Bill Speidel

Seattle, Washington
Nettle Creek Publishing Company 1978

FIRST EDITION

CIP Library of Congress Cataloging in Publication Data

Speidel, William C.   1912-

    Doc Maynard : the man who invented Seattle

    Bibliography: p.
    Includes index.
    1. Maynard, David Swinson, 1808-1873.   2. Seattle—Biography
    3. Seattle—History   4. Physicians—Washington (State)—
       Seattle—Biography.
    I. Title.   II. Title: The Man Who Invented Seattle.

F899.S453 M397   979.7'77   78-10146
ISBN 0-914890-02-6

International Standard Book Number 0-914890-02-6

Library of Congress Catalog Card Number 7810146

Copyright © 1978 by William C. Speidel

Nettle Creek Publishing Company
600 First Avenue—Suite 310
Seattle, Washington 98104

Printed in the United States of America
by George Banta Company, Inc., Menasha, Wisconsin

A SPECIAL TRIBUTE TO THE OMBUDSWOMAN

The reader owes a debt of magnificent proportions to SHIRLEY PORRO, who served as ombudswoman in this manuscript. She cut through the red tape and got down to the meat of the coconut. And all of us should be thankful. I'd look like an idiot and the reader would have been hopelessly confused in and among the fascinating side trips that didn't have anything to do with either Doc Maynard or the invention of Seattle.

Also by Bill Speidel

You Can't Eat Mt. Rainier!— *(1955—out of print)*

Be My Guest! In the Pacific Northwest *(1957—out of print)*

You *Still* Can't Eat Mt. Rainier! *(1961—out of print)*

Sons of the Profits—Seattle Story 1851-1901
   (1st Ed. 1967, 9th printing 1978)

The Wet Side of the Mountains *(1st ed., 1974)*

It Was a Hell of a Blast! *(1975)*

David Swinson Maynard

"So I went down to my cabin pretty mad
and climbed into the sack and read a
lesson in my Correspondence Course on
American history, but I didn't find a thing
there to cheer me up—it was the same
selection of bums we have today, only
they wore funny clothes and had never
heard of bubble gum."

Richard Bissell, *High Water*

TABLE OF CONTENTS

LIST OF ILLUSTRATIONS

I

Doc

A book called *Sons of the Profits,* which I wrote a decade ago, starts out with: "I'm sure there must have been *somebody* who participated in the construction of Seattle without first determining whether there was a buck in it for himself, but this book isn't about him."

During the intervening years, I found the somebody . . .

And this book *is* about him.

His name was David Swinson Maynard.

He was a licensed medical doctor. At the age of forty-four, he was half again as old and a thousand times more knowledgeable than the backwoods folk who generally have been credited with founding our town. And (this one will visit heart attacks upon a lot of our present citizens) he patterned it after Cleveland, Ohio.

If the men in *Profits* could have made more money by *not* building a city, then that's what they would have done. But the doctor invented a money-making machine. The profiteers just used it. In *Profits,* I said, "Seattle lucked out on a lot of things, the most important of which was her geographic location in the center of the Sound."

Doc Maynard put Seattle where she is on purpose!

Historian Hubert H. Bancroft wrote that "the rage for laying out towns (in the Pacific Northwest) was at its height between 1850 and 1852." Doc Maynard's shrewd intelligence was in competition with at least twenty-five other men who were trying to come up with the most important city in the northwest at that same time.

1

Portland was the one that gave him the best run for his money. It had a population of 2,000 when he got Seattle going. It would take fifty years for Seattle to forge ahead. And we did it by simply cranking the machinery the doctor had invented.

He was monarch of all he surveyed—and what some of the others surveyed as well—for the first seven years of Seattle's existence. And as he bent the twig, the city grew for the next fifty years . . . until the Christers took over and passed the State's 1909 Blue Laws, which made anything that was fun illegal.

Concomitant with the invention of Seattle, the doctor created what has become our state out of the massive Oregon Territory . . . and won King County as kind of a booby prize.

Doctor Maynard was the first person to call Seattle the "Queen City of the Pacific Northwest," and "The Gateway to the Orient." He put Seattle on the map of the United States as the terminus of the transcontinental railroad. He was the first resident to recognize the importance of Snoqualmie Pass, which is the lowest pass in the Cascades.

He named the town. He brought the first residents here . . . the first store . . . pharmacy . . . restaurant . . . hotel . . . gambling joint . . . saloon and whorehouse.

It was his specific ambition to make Seattle the greatest city on earth.

Today, the viable essence of our town is the same as it was 126 years ago when he slapped the baby's bottom and delivered her, squalling and protesting, to the rest of the world.

And, oh, yes, he had one other thing going for him that too often is missing today . . .

A magnificent sense of humor.

A man called Maynard

There are a lot of people with medical degrees whom you wouldn't dare call "Doc." It would injure their dignity . . . a dignity that is at best precarious. But Doctor Maynard was of the earth earthy.

He rolled through life like a solid gold ball, without worrying that somebody else might scratch the surface and find it was just gilt paint.

He loved to tell the story of a couple of his progenitors, a Maynard and a Swinson, who were picked up by a British press gang and lodged aboard a warship at the start of the American Revolutionary War. When they protested, they were informed that their services were required to put down the revolution. When they continued to protest, their clothes were removed and they were tossed in the brig.

That night they broke out of the brig, jumped overboard and swam ashore. To the astonishment of a townswoman, they appeared at her door inquiring as to the shortest route to General George Washington's camp. They presented themselves in their long johns to George, himself. And they fought at his side throughout the war.

Throughout his years, the doctor carried on the tradition of the two young men who had presented themselves to General Washington. He liked their spirit, enjoyed telling that story, and incorporated that kind of thing in his own life. Most of the people he met in the Pacific Northwest got a kick out of him. But the Christers—who were the ones he fought with during his invention of our town—were horrified. And I have to believe that he did a lot of the things he did for the pure pleasure of throwing them into a tailspin.

How can you call anybody like that anything but "Doc?"

Little is said in our current history books about him before he got to the Pacific Northwest. But the truth is that he had made and gone through two fortunes before he arrived here. And then he set about building his third and using it for the construction of his town.

He was older than anybody else who participated in the original construction of our town . . . nearly twice the age of some of the men who played key roles. The creation of a new town represented a chance to start life all over again when most of his contemporaries long since had gone to their rewards.

Doc Maynard was a man with a powerful physique. He hovered around six feet in height. He had the shoulders of a lineman on a

professional football team, sloping to a strong neck. He had curly
black hair, a broad forehead, wide set china blue eyes and a promi-
nent nose, wide mouth and squared, determined chin . . . powerful
arms with hands that could be as gentle as a whisper when the need
arose. His was an elongated torso on top of legs that were as sturdy as
fenceposts . . . a weight-lifter of championship proportions.

Physically, there was nothing he didn't think he could do—and
usually did it . . . to the astonishment of those around him . . . even
in a society that was highly "physical" to begin with. Only once did he
use his strength to chastise another living creature—and I suspect she
had it coming.

The doctor detested violence.

If there was one outstanding characteristic, this was it. If at all possible,
he avoided confrontations. He manipulated people as a matter of
personal preference and I doubt that ever, in his whole life, did he let
his right hand know what his left hand was doing.

The doctor was a highly emotional man who threw himself completely
into any project he felt required his attention. Thomas Prosch, his
principal biographer, said: "There was no holding back with him. If a
thing was desirable he was in favor of it; if wanted, he would go
at once; if it had to be done or it was well to do it, he was ready to
devote to it his money to the last dollar."

That's the man who invented Seattle.

The man and the medicine

Born on March 22, 1808, near the town of Castleton, Vermont,
David Swinson Maynard gobbled up the necessities of preparatory
education by the time he was seventeen years old and showed such
bright promise that he was accepted as a student at Castleton Medical
School. Unlike a lot of other medical schools in those days it had
a solid foundation in legitimate medical education and subsequently
became the medical school at Middlebury College.

As was his wont on any project during his entire life, he went about
learning what there was know about the practice of medicine flat-
out, full-speed-ahead and no-holds-barred. And being top man in

his class, he got the coveted position as apprentice to one Dr. Theodore Woodward, professor of obstetrics and surgery and the most important teacher in the school.

You have to keep in mind that in those days getting a medical degree was not exactly the same process people go through today. Whatever formal education he got, he got by the time he was twenty years old. With the possible exception of Philadelphia and New York, the medical schools were operated privately. The free enterprise system ran rampant. For as little as fifty bucks and a six-months correspondence school course, a butcher could put the name "doctor" in front of his own . . . and a lot of them did. At best a man—and there were very few women—blew about $500 and three years of his time in some kind of medical institution. This included his room and board. And he could get into medical school right out of high school.

These schools were only supplementary, however, for the backbone of medical education then was preceptorship, the American form of Europe's apprentice system. The student kept the doctor's office clean, compounded the powders and salves, and looked after the horses, in return for the use of his preceptor's library and the privilege of watching him in the task of examining and prescribing.

A book about the Mayo Brothers notes that, "When an alert young mind, observant, curious and full of questions, met with a seasoned practitioner, able and willing to impart the wisdom he had gained from his years of experience, preceptorship was a reasonably satisfactory form of medical education, certainly far superior to classroom lectures alone."

There wasn't a drug store at every corner of America as there is today. The doctor had to gather his own roots and berries, plant his own herb garden in his own back yard.

And when the doctor came west, he brought the seeds for his herbs with him. There's the story of one man who nurtured a small tree all the way across the Great American Desert—doing without water himself so he could keep his specimen alive. And what did he bring to the Pacific Northwest? A fir tree. Doc Maynard had his own variation of the same thing. He was using dandelions as a diuretic and laxative and brought some seeds of this flower with him . . .

Only to discover cascara bark when he got here.

Calomel was big in his black bag. A mercurous chloride, it was used as a purgative and fungicide, along with another mercuric compound called "blue mass." At any rate, these were the ones which cropped up with the greatest frequency in the diary he kept on the Oregon Trail. Sulphur and molasses were a part of his thing . . . soda and soap.

Soap was big with the doctor.

He used it himself with great regularity—and he required those around him to use it, too . . . a custom that got him into no end of trouble among the hardy westerners who took a bath once a year—and then only if they felt they really needed it. Doctor Maynard was an oddball who took a bath once a week whether he needed it or not—and washed his hands and face several times a day.

Whatever else he got out of his medical education is somewhat hazy, but he sure got habits of cleanliness that lasted him a lifetime. He also acquired the costume of a doctor. It was on occasions so rare that historians made special mention of it that he failed to appear in public immaculately clad in white linen, black suit and vest.

Malaria was called the "ague" in those days—and there was plenty of it around the Pacific Northwest. Fortunately, the doctor had a specific for it in quinine. He also had ipecac, which induces vomiting. And both of these would play their own major roles in the creation and development of Seattle—along with what the doctors, the patent medicine people and just about everybody else called "tonic."

The active ingredient of tonic was opium. The resulting state of genial euphoria made them think they were better, whether or not they in fact were. It was used with the careless abandon of the aspirin tablet of today, and it was cheaper than booze.

For instance, when Sears, Roebuck & Co. got going half a century or so after the doctor got his medical education, you could buy opium-based tonic through the catalogue at $2.50 a pint. By 1900, America was a nation of opium addicts.

At any rate, opium as a tonic, and dissolved in alcohol and called laudanum, was a major part of the doctor's little black bag . . . perhaps too major a part. On the other hand, it was too major a part of the black bag of any doctor in the world. Doc Maynard was an obsessive enemy of pain. And opium often was the only weapon he had.

The final result of Doctor Maynard's medical training was Seattle's first hospital, which he founded in 1863 and in which he practiced medicine as he thought it ought to be practiced. Once more, Prosch provides us with proper insights: "As a physician Seattle had no better during his time. He was one of the olden school, not the modern, which relies too much upon surgery, upon the use of the knife and the saw. Nor was he a great medicine doser. He depended largely upon the most simple means—upon pleasant surroundings, a cheerful atmosphere, confidence on the part of the patient, the alleviation of pain, fresh air, sanitary conditions, and an occasional bit of pardonable deception. Many a person who imagined himself or herself dangerously ill was cured by him with a prescription of water, disguised, perhaps, by the addition of salt or other harmless ingredient."

That's a thumbnail sketch of the first successful physician in the city of Seattle . . . and it's not a bad description of what a physician ought to be doing today.

But we also fell heir to something else that happened to the doctor about the time he was twenty years old . . . shortly before he graduated, and before he could serve his internship with Dr. Woodward.

He fell in love.

The phantom lady

He did it with the same intensity that marked everything else in his life, and that episode provides us with a further insight into his personality.

There are a lot of men, and women, too, for that matter, who practice the philosophy that if they can't be near the one that they love they will love the one they are near. Many of his friends, for instance, flitted from one love affair to another. But the doctor was not of this genre.

He was a one-woman-at-a-time man.

History records two of the women, but the third—who really was the first—probably will always remain as the phantom lady. At any rate, while he still was a medical student, he succumbed to a pair of beautiful brown eyes . . .

Or were they blue?

It doesn't matter.

What does matter is that he fell very hard and the young lady in question put him to the first tough decision of his young life. She wouldn't wait for him to get his license to practice medicine. If he would give up his medical career and go to work she would marry him. If not, too bad.

She was a beautiful young woman and sought after by a number of other young men. The doctor had to choose between her and his medical career. It cut him up something awful, but he chose the medical career. It was a choice between love and medicine and he chose the latter . . .

A bitter pill which he never forgot . . .

The choice was between his head and his heart.

He chose his head . . . and lost the girl.

Years later, when he was confronted with a similar situation, he took the opposite course. You make the best decision you can at any given moment. And that's the way he played both of these decisions. He was right and he was wrong in both, but without them he would not have brought the city of Seattle as we now know it into existence. Somebody else might have created "a" city. But it wouldn't have been "our" Seattle.

That, however, is the long range look.

The phantom lady initiated a not unprecedented course in human events known as "marrying on the rebound."

The perfidy of Lydia A. Rickey

Doc Maynard made the biggest mistake of his life on August 28, 1828 . . .

Her name was Lydia A. Rickey . . .

Doc did not leave a lot of progeny around the Pacific Northwest to extol his virtues—either real or fancied. He had his own built-in ego, so he didn't have to go around rubbing other peoples' noses in an imaginary concept of his importance. Although he was an emotional man who usually let his emotions dictate his actions, this time he used his head. In those days, family ties were big in the doctor's life. The Maynards and the Swinsons were long time friends. Prosch says, "The two families lived in the same neighborhood, fought in the same wars, educated and reared their children together, intermarried, and otherwise associated in the many ways incident to the life and times of the eighteenth century, first in the British province and later in the young American possession and state in which their lot had been cast . . ."

In the same bunch was the Rickey family.

Lydia Rickey was a part of his peer group. He was twenty. The first great love of his life had told him to go jump in the lake. And there was Lydia . . . member of a fine family . . . approved by his peers. She came from fine stock. How could he go wrong letting her be the mother of his children? He wasn't in love with Lydia, but look what love had done to him.

It's too bad we trust something as difficult as marriage to the young.

Anyway, they were "properly" married, and it ended up providing a permanent cure of "propriety" with the doctor.

He never would be "proper" again after Lydia.

Very properly the young couple produced a daughter, Frances, in 1830, and a son, Henry, in 1834.

The closest we can come to the next important date is April, 1841. The doctor was out making a call on a patient. And if you'd like to make a comparison between today and those days, he got four-bits for house calls—two-bits for office treatments. No wonder doctors turned their talents to other enterprises . . . you could buy a doctor or five pounds of pork chops for fifty cents.

Anyway, here's how the story goes in an affidavit which the doctor signed under oath a decade later: "That in the month of April of the year last aforesaid (1841) on returning home from visiting a patient at about the hour of ten o'clock in the night—found his wife lying with a certain John Hemrick in an obscene manner. That the undersigned had previously doubted her chastity but had never before seen anything positively confirming his suspicions . . ."

There's really no point in going into detail about the perfidy of Lydia except to note that the various documents introduced into the doctor's affidavit would indicate that Lydia had been sleeping with every available man in Cleveland, Ohio, at the time. Not only was she sleeping around, she was proud of her record. One of the great quotes in the records came from a witness who saw Lydia "kissing Ormsby and that, too, in the bushes."

In view of the fact that she and the doctor no longer were in love with one another—and as far as the doctor was concerned a deep and passionate attachment never had been part of the picture—it's hard to fault Lydia for infidelity.

Stupidity, yes.

Promiscuity, yes.

But infidelity . . .

The doctor had that one coming.

It's the doctor's reaction to this traumatic confrontation which is important in this book. He still was hidebound by convention—an ailment from which he recovered with maturity. In those days there were two clearcut grounds for divorce: adultery and desertion. If the doctor had marched out of the house and into court with the adultery charge, he would have saved himself a lot of financial trouble later on. He was sore enough at Lydia to do it. But, as he testified later, he couldn't do it to her family. The disgrace would have destroyed their standing in the community and he couldn't bring himself to do that to them.

And then there were the children. He had to preserve the marriage for the sake of the children . . . what a fallacy!

Also, under his code of ethics, he had to leave Lydia with what he called "a sufficient competence."

Let's see, the children were eleven and seven at the time. The doctor stuck around for the next nine years . . . until Frances was twenty . . . and Henry was sixteen. What a friendly atmosphere there was in that family; the doctor grimly trying to put together that damned "competence," and Lydia out sleeping with anybody she could get to lay hands on her.

Great family unit.

By 1850, the doctor acquired the "competence" he was aiming for. This included a home that he could give to Lydia and a pile of money big enough that, properly invested, would enable her to live comfortably for the rest of her life. But her idea of comfort tended more toward things like kissing Ormsby in the bushes. She never remarried. She just hung around where she later could make the most possible trouble for the doctor.

On the other hand, knowing something about her helps us understand him. In later years, when he had mellowed some on the subject, he opined that while she had been sleeping with every man in Cleveland, it wasn't a very big town at the time.

Blueprint for Seattle

For nearly a hundred years now, a place called Cherry Grove, Illinois, has been rammed down our children's throats as the place from which our pioneer forefathers originated . . . and presumably they built a town out here just like the one they had left back there.

It's going to come as something of a surprise to everyone concerned— especially to the people who write the history books for the Seattle Public School system—that Cleveland, Ohio, is the town after which Seattle is patterned, not Cherry Grove.

For most people, Cleveland is the last place on earth they would like to live.

Last place?

Well, not quite the last. Los Angeles is the *last*. Then come Pittsburgh, Chicago and New York. But Cleveland is right up there in the top ten. A lot of folks living here today are fugitives from Cleveland. There's a certain stuffy side to Seattle that reminds us of Cleveland, but we can put our minds to rest on that subject. The stuffy side of Seattle came from Cherry Grove. Cherry Grove went to sleep one night about a century ago, and never woke up. If you want to see what Seattle would have been like if it had been patterned after Cherry Grove, you'll have to take a trip to Port Gamble on the Olympic Peninsula where the Pope & Talbot people have restored the sleepy little lumber town that used to be there.

Cleveland, at least, as the third largest city in the country, is alive and well.

And Maynard was a fugitive from Cleveland.

He and a whole collection of Swinsons, Maynards and Rickeys had joined a general migration to the Western Reserve, in which Cleveland is located, some time in the early 1830's. For the next eighteen years or so, he would dedicate to Cleveland the same overboard enthusiasm he gave to any project he got into . . . and would make and dispose of two fortunes in the process.

To calm the nerves of people who might be concerned about this kind of thing, Cleveland did not develop into a steel town until after the doctor left there is 1850. During his time there, it was a major distribution center, a lot like Seattle is today. And he picked up a lot of good ideas there which you will find that he used in the invention of Seattle.

For instance, the town fathers made significant attempts to bring in a good "mix" of people. If a man was a good doctor, or a good dentist, or a good blacksmith, carpenter or plumber, he could get an excellent deal on a piece of real estate . . . for twenty-five or fifty bucks, he could buy a town lot.

Had to build on it, however, or it would be repossessed. Doc Maynard would use that one with telling effect in the invention of Seattle.

A device which we find commonplace or even passe today was unique in 1836 when it was introduced in Cleveland. Crowds collected around to look at it in a department store window . . . and there were headlines in the newspaper reading:

"Bathtub arrives in Cleveland!"

You could get in this thing and get wet all over and wash your whole body. To the impressionable young doctor, with whom cleanliness ran well ahead of Godliness—causing him no end of trouble then and in the future—this was the answer to a prayer. Some of those devices even had hot and cold water piped right in!

Another idea which the doctor applied to Puget Sound was the layout of the town and the inclusion in the original plat of a forty-four-acre town square in the center of the plat.

He got another lesson from the bloody battles that were fought between Cleveland and Ohio City, on the other side of the river. The towns ultimately were merged and a whole lot of hard feeling could have been avoided if they had worked together from the beginning. It made an impression on the doctor, and when the chips were down in Seattle, he saw to it that this kind of thing was avoided on Elliott Bay.

The combination of coal and iron ore to create steel was just coming into Cleveland when the doctor left, and in those days, it was a marriage devoutly sought after by any town father. The age of steel was upon the nation. Steel tracks soon would connect the two coasts of this country. Steel steam locomotives would run along those tracks. Coal would provide the fuel for the locomotives and for the steel steamships that soon would connect this continent with other continents of the world.

Doc would waste a lot of time trying to find the combination of iron and steel for his town. But it was only natural. Shortly after his arrival in Cleveland, the first foundry to use steam instead of horsepower for "blowing" was developed. The first locomotive west of the

Alleghenies was built. The forerunners of the New York Central and the Pennsylvania railroads were initiated here.

Cleveland had forged ahead as a trading center because of the canal systems between the east coast and the Great Lakes. But the railroads were replacing them and the doctor made his first fortune investing in railroading. The city of Cleveland encouraged this kind of thing by extending the town's credit for incredible sums of money for those times, like a quarter of a million dollars. Cleveland history relates it like this: "Among the incorporators were men of leadership and vision. A charter was granted in the heat of the speculative period (1836) providing for banking powers and the issuance of paper money, as well as the right to build the railroad . . . Stupendous engineering plans called for the driving of a double row of piles on which rested stringers . . . the expense of grading would thus be saved by utilizing this elaborate stilt system . . ."

Shades of Cleveland in Seattle.

The first railroad arrived here on such a stilt system.

One day, the doctor had a net worth of $30,000 in railroading—the equivalent of $300,000 in today's money. The next day (in the panic of 1837) he was $30,000 in the hole when the railroad went belly-up and because he had co-signed a note with somebody else.

This gives us an insight into Maynard's standing in Cleveland.

How many men in Seattle today can get $300,000 on only their personal signature?

The bankers didn't lose by this, either. The other guy blew town . . . Doc Maynard stayed around to make another fortune, pay off the note . . . pay off Lydia and leave town.

In this connection, Doc Maynard, who would try nearly anything once, got into the Medical School business with one Dr. Horace Ackley. It was Cleveland's first and became the forerunner of the medical school at Western Reserve University. At one time the two young men had 150 students paying something like $200 a year tuition. A proprietary school, it was a going business that dropped dead in the panic of 1837 . . . losing a bundle for Maynard, but Doc regained it and more before he left thirteen years later.

When the doctor arrived in Cleveland, it had a population of 500. By the time he left, it had grown to 17,000 . . . and it had two medical schools . . . a university . . . a homeopathic institute . . . an academy of natural sciences . . . a Roman Catholic Cathedral . . . the famous Case Library. It was a medical, cultural, literary and musical center. It had gaslight, planked roads, banks, churches, industry, commercial enterprises, gambling joints, whorehouses, saloons and railroads.

Cleveland's development resulted from the fact that it was the major crossroads of the mid-west at the time. It was built at the mouth of a meandering river called the Cuyahoga, which emptied into a large body of water called Lake Erie. Canals and then railroads built her into a major town, but in the original instance its prominence resulted from a simple economic fact . . .

The town's hinterland became the breadbasket for the little villages springing up all around Lake Erie. The town, itself, became the center of trade for the lake.

What the doctor looked for when he finally got to the Pacific Northwest was a good site at the mouth of a river that furnished transportation for the products of a rich hinterland to a large body of water where there were small towns which needed those products.

The town also should be the logical location of the terminus of a transcontinental railroad which the doctor believed would be materializing "any day now."

The doctor participated as an active businessman in Cleveland for eighteen years . . . from 1832 to 1850 . . . and by the time he left that location he was thoroughly acquainted with all of the aspects of putting together a major city.

II

It was a tough fuckin' trip

The Oregon Trail and the people who crossed it in wagon trains during the quarter of a century beginning in 1841, have combined to become kind of a religious cult in the Pacific Northwest. I went to a meeting of the Daughters of the Pioneers in Seattle, for instance, and the people there were wearing badges showing the mode of transportation used by their progenitors in getting here. If your ancestor came in a covered wagon, you sat at the head table. If he or she came by train, you could hardly get in the front door.

A lot of movies show the Indians whacking away at the emigrants, but the record massacre, done by a party of Mormons dressed like Indians at Mountain Meadows on September 11, 1857, puts the Indians to shame. Although the raid was not sponsored by the church, the raiders killed 120 people, sparing only the lives of seventeen children under the age of seven. I wouldn't get into the Mormon thing but for the fact that during his trip through Mormon territory, Doc Maynard stayed awake every night, guarding his people after performing incredible feats of strength all day on the trail itself.

Thanks to the Mormons, we know what an iron man Doc was.

But the real fatalities that go to make up the statistics of about a thousand people a year who died on that trail were perpetrated by the people participating in the trip. They tried one another and hung the guilty parties from a couple of wagon tongues stuck up in the air.

They hadn't the slightest idea of antisepsis—and cared even less—and died by the thousands during the cholera epidemics.

Ignorance and sheer stupidity did most of them in. They drove off cliffs. They drowned in rivers. They starved to death. A huge percentage drove their animals to death—which is where Doc Maynard broke his pick with the people on his own wagon train. They quarreled among themselves. They had a terrible time with their leaders. Usually, the guys who started out as leaders got fired before the trip was well under way. This was truer of the people who came to the Pacific Northwest than the ones who went to California. The men who organized the trips to California during the gold rush were well-heeled, tough men who financed wagon trains themselves and didn't brook insolence on the part of those who went along for the ride.

For the most part, the people who came to Oregon were the ones who rode steerage instead of first class on the river boats to St. Joseph and Independence, Missouri. They were the dirt farmers who weren't making it where they were, or they wouldn't have come west in the first place. They were the ones who said their prayers every night and twice on Sundays.

Many really didn't have the least concept of what they were up to and today they couldn't get a driver's license. The most shocking example was that of the guy who was driving along the trail with a loaded and cocked rifle in his lap. It accidentally was discharged and he blew the head off the baby in her mother's arms in the next wagon.

In our day, we seem to equate the trail to one of the transcontinental freeways, but it wasn't like that at all. Writing about it, our most professional pioneer, Ezra Meeker, of Puyallup, tells about crossing the Missouri where wagons were starting four abreast with oxen of one wagon breathing on the tailgate of the one ahead. "I realized it was like this for 500 miles ahead of me."

The emigration started with the arrival of grass in the spring and hundreds of thousands of animals depended on that grass to get the people across the country. Without grass, nobody moved. So, instead of being a four or six-lane highway, the trail was about a hundred miles wide.

Granted they had a tough time, but it wasn't all bad. Those who survived didn't have to take any sleeping pills to get a night's rest. A lot of sickly people got well—or died—in the process. And you didn't have to coax the kids to eat their breakfast cereal. Doc Maynard had his fair share of troubles. And fortunately for someone who wanted to find out what kind of a guy he was, he kept a diary. He was not what you could call a prolific writer, but his casual dismissals of events of heroic proportions are in themselves an indication of what kind of man he was. (He didn't even include his closest brush with death, which came at the end of the trip.)

On the other hand, he had a premarital, transcontinental honeymoon with the woman he loved. That wouldn't raise many eyebrows today, but it sure did then . . . and it sure had a lot to do with the history of our town.

Actuarially speaking, the doctor had a life expectancy of thirty-five years when he was born. So, he should have been pushing up daisies for seven years before he even started west. He was forty-two years old at the time . . . starting a new life and inventing Seattle before he died at the age of sixty-five.

"Took the cars to Sandusky . . ."

On Tuesday, April 9, 1850, Doc Maynard entered the following in the diary he kept during his trip across the United States and for a month intermittently after he reached the Pacific Northwest: "Left home for California. Passed through Norwalk to Monroeville. Took the cars to Sandusky . . . passage 75 cents."

The above, as well as the rest of the diary he kept on his transcontinental trek, needs to be fleshed out for full understanding.

He wasn't really *going* to California.

What he was doing was *leaving* Cleveland.

Where he was going didn't really matter. He might, for instance, have left Cleveland for Columbus two years earlier if his candidate for governor of Ohio, John B. Weller, had not lost by the slimmest margin of votes in Ohio history—311 votes out of 297,201 votes cast.

The doctor had played a major role backstage in that campaign and would have been named to Weller's "cabinet" if he had won.

Weller was the one who finally talked Maynard into leaving Ohio for California, and it always has been assumed that the doctor was headed west for the gold rush. But Weller had a healthy selfishness that reached above and beyond a mundane desire to see the doctor get rich. He wanted to be the first United States Senator from California, where he had gone after his unsuccessful attempt at the Ohio governorship. He offered the doctor a pot of gold in exchange for Maynard's services as a master politician in his senatorial campaign.

For two years, construction of the new Cleveland, Columbus & Cincinnati railroad had absorbed the community. Three weeks before, the Cleveland City Council had officially opened the first fifteen mile stretch. Cleveland history says: "Behind the proud little locomotive, its high, expanded stack belching billows of smoke, they bounded adventurously over that distance in the remarkable time of twenty-seven minutes. Civic pride ran high, and as a humorist observed, the locomotive (The Cleveland) was the only 'motive' that could induce a man to leave Cleveland."

Doc, of course, had yet another motive. Her name was Lydia.

Nonetheless, it was a trip which excited him. The brass-trimmed, wood-burning locomotive moved on a pair of six-foot drivers and four front wheels. It had no cow-catcher or headlight, but it made the most of its shrill whistle. Behind the engine was a boxlike car piled high with wood, followed by the watertender and three forty-foot passenger cars with quaint curtains, railed platforms and handrails . . .

And speed?

Man . . .

It did an incredible twenty miles an hour.

One day people would take the "cars" all the way to California!

Life begins at forty-two

Doctor Maynard's "reincarnation" was into its second month and seventh day on May 16, 1850, in St. Joseph, Missouri, when he made an actuality of his theory about the cheapest way of getting his body across the United States. He had a mule, a buffalo robe, a gun, his precious medicines, his surgical instruments and several volumes of advice on the pitfalls and possibilities of transcontinental travel.

Some 50,000 people would emigrate from St. Joseph and Independence, Missouri, to the west coast of America the year that Doctor Maynard took the trail . . . with about 49,000 of them headed for the gold diggings in California, and the others to Oregon Territory where a single man or woman could get 320 acres of rich agricultural land, although there was beginning to be talk of prosperity to be derived from cutting down a vast crop of timber and shipping it to California.

A spirit of optimism was in the air in St. Joseph.

The town was crowded. A multitude of shops had sprung up to cater to the needs of the emigrants. There was an incessant hammering and banging from a dozen blacksmith shops where the wagons were being prepared or repaired, the horses and oxen shod. The streets thronged with men, horses and mules. Supplies for the emigrant trains over-flowed from the shops to the streets. Saloons were booming. Houses of ill repute echoed to the songs of pleasure far into the night, while on the prairie surrounding the town there was a continuation of the confusion as the emigrants for Oregon, who were largely sober and God-fearing, were holding meetings . . . passing resolutions . . . establishing regulations—and having an awful time trying to choose a wagon master.

As a general thing, the people heading for the gold rush in California held themselves aloof from the Oregon immigrants. Many of them were persons of wealth and standing. They were the ones who stayed at the best hotels, provided the gunsmiths and saddlers with patronage for the best equipment. They had arrived here in the first class section of the riverboats and looked down on the travelers bound for Oregon Territory who, in general, had counted themselves lucky to arrive in steerage. In the California group were the speculators, adventurers, gamblers.

With his qualifications as a medical man, it was easy for Doc Maynard to make a connection with the best equipped and managed

California-bound wagon train in the town . . . which he did immediately upon his arrival. And, on May 16, the party with which he had associated himself crossed the Missouri River and encamped.

The travelers from St. Joseph would join with those from Independence at the confluence of the Big and Little Blue rivers in Kansas. They would follow the Little Blue to Fort Kearney, Nebraska, where they would transfer their affections to the North Platte River to Independence, Wyoming, and picking up the Sweetwater River as far as South Pass through the Rocky Mountains. On the west side of the Rockies, the vast majority of the immigrants would head for California . . . which was the doctor's plan.

The man and the cholera

The first inkling of the disease which would change the course of Doc Maynard's life and lead to the invention of Seattle appears with this cursory notation in his diary on May 19, 1850, slightly less than two years before he would stake his claim in what we now know as the Pioneer Square Historic District. The entry reads: "Passed one grave." The next day he notes that he "passed some new graves." Then comes this: "May 21—Tuesday. Passed the grave of A. Powers, of Peoria County, Illinois, died on the 20th inst., about sixty-five miles west of St. Joseph. Traveled eighteen miles. Was called to visit three cases of cholera. One died, a man leaving a wife and child, from Illinois, poor. He lived seven hours after being taken. No wood or water secured."

There are a lot of ways to go . . .

But cholera is not the most pleasant.

It begins suddenly, with terrific purging. The victim has no control over his bowels or his vomiting. The combination of the two creates cramps and prostration. In many instances, apparently healthy people drop in their tracks as though felled by an invisible club. Within hours, the patient loses most of his body fluids . . . like eight to ten quarts in a period of twenty-four hours. His eyes become sunken and the skin clings to the bones, giving the victim the appearance of a living skeleton. Of particular horror is the fact that the patient remains lucid . . . realizes he's about to die.

Today the treatment consists of massive doses of liquids—as one doctor notes, "gallons, not pints"—intravenously. Cholera originally appeared in India and the Orient where the British doctors, for their own reasons, believed that all liquids must be withheld from the victims . . . even to the extent that sentries were placed at the entrances to the hospitals lest some kind-hearted nurse might smuggle in a little water to the patients who were screaming for it.

Nobody clicked that it was a communicable disease. Its incidence was blamed on electricity in the air . . . on swamps . . . on watermelons . . . tomatoes . . . cucumbers. In America the Christians were convinced that it was a scourge in the hand of God, striking down heathens.

It would never appear in our God-fearing society.

Then, in 1832, it crossed the Atlantic, following the channels of trade, and penetrated the United States . . . bringing panic with it. (The doctor was four years out of medical school at the time.) It hit Cleveland the hardest two years later when there were 100 deaths in a town with a population of about 2,000 . . . and that was minor alongside of nearby Cincinnati which lost twenty per cent of its population . . . or New Orleans where 5,000 deaths were reported.

The doctor was never one to participate in the activities of any church, but he was totally turned off by the Protestants' approach to the solution of the problem. They figured that if the President of the United States would declare a day of fasting and prayer, we could lick the disease right now. They believed this was a wrathful deity ridding the premises of sinners.

Doc Maynard believed the disease struck people who had to live in squalid conditions and didn't have enough proper food to eat. It was this epidemic that turned him away from the trappings of the Protestant faith and caused him to join the Masons, a group that would be enhanced by his enthusiasm for the rest of his life.

The American medical profession went through what now is termed the "dark ages of medicine" in this country during the cholera years here—from 1832 to 1834, and in 1849 and 1850. A doctor was left to his own devices to try anything he wanted. One that you may not want to read about was the practice of fastening an electrode to the base of the patient's neck and another up his rectum and turning on the juice from a galvanic battery.

The doctors complained that the patients objected strenuously, but the treatment was continued for five or six hours.

The result was death.

The most ingenious treatment was that of a doctor who provided the patient with a tobacco smoke enema, accompanied by a beeswax plug . . . at least symbolic of the fact that the medical profession was blowing smoke up the patients' asses.

Cholera was particularly frightening on the Oregon Trail. Charles Rosenberg wrote: "Cholera waited in the brackish streams and water-holes, left by one party, to be passed on to the next group following across the plains. The route westward was marked with wooden crosses and stone cairns, the crosses often bearing only a name and 'cholera.' Nowhere could the disease have been more terrifying than on those trails, where men died without physicians, without ministers and without friends."

The wooden grave markers on the trail have aptly been described as a broken picket fence. People died of a lot of things on the Oregon Trail, but none died with more terror than the victims of cholera. Estimates of the number of deaths from this cause run as high as 20,000.

Commenting on the treatment of cholera in the United States in 1850, one of the leading authorities on the disease in the World Health Organization in Geneva, Switzerland, said, "Your chances of surviving an attack were about as good as though you had been shot in the stomach at point-blank range . . . maybe fifty per cent. On the other hand, if you fell into the hands of the average doctor your chance of dying rose to about ninety per cent."

To Doc Maynard, fresh from treating the 1849 epidemic in Cleveland, the incidence of cholera was as commonplace as the common cold. His principal weapon was calomel. On two occasions, he contracted the disease himself. And he was in such excellent physical condition that he threw off both attacks with self-administered calomel . . . which at least had a tendency to sterilize the bowels.

The doctor's treatment consisted of keeping the patients warm and comfortable . . . boiling all the water that anybody drank and providing the patients with as much tea as he could persuade them to swallow. And finally, he had opium. It didn't do much beyond relaxing the affected organs of the body as far as treating the patient was concerned.

But it eased his passage to the beyond.

If we got as much as a single case of cholera in Seattle today, it would make headlines in all media throughout the world. There hasn't been a case of cholera in the United States in half a century.

In the three weeks following his call to the first patient, Doc Maynard was summoned to the sides of thirty-five cholera victims. He saved about two thirds of them . . .

Which was spectacular success for the state of the art at that time.

Panic on the plains

On June 3 the doctor wrote: "Fell in with innumerable hosts of immigrants. Rained through the night." The next day he wrote: "Traveled up the Platte River twenty miles. The road was low, level, muddy. The river is about a mile wide. At 2 o'clock it began to rain and blow tremendously, continuing all night. Camped without a spark of fire or warm supper, with our clothes as wet as water. A man died within sight of us. He was a Mason. I was called to see him, but too late . . ."

Writing of the same conditions at about the same place and the same time of year, historian Francis Parkman Jr. fills out the picture with: "The thunder here is not like the tame thunder of the Atlantic coast. Bursting with a terrific crash just above our heads, it roared over the boundless waste of prairie, seeming to roll around the whole circle of the firmament with a peculiar and awful reverberation. The lightning flashed all night, played with its livid glare upon the neighboring trees, revealing the vast expanse of the plain, and then leaving us shut in as by a palpable wall of darkness . . .

"We lay upon India-rubber cloths, placed between our blankets and the soil. For a while they excluded the water to admiration; but when at length it accumulated and began to run over the edges, they served equally well to retain it, so toward the end of the night we were unconsciously reposing in small pools of rain."

It rained steadily for three days and nights.

Doc witnessed three more cholera deaths.

On June seventh the doctor awakened, still wet, to another lowering sky in a desolate land dominated by massive sheets of water . . . grass trampled by the hoofs of thousands of animals and of wagon wheels.

A messenger came from a stricken wagon train, his face pale and agitated. A whole bunch of people were dying. Would the doctor come?

The other members of the doctor's party would have no part of any more cholera. "You stay here and you stay alone," the wagon master said. "We're leaving."

The doctor detached himself from his party, following the panic-stricken messenger through the sea of mud.

He had embarked on a journey that would end with the founding of the city of Seattle.

A tale of two sisters

Hans Christian Andersen's story about the Ugly Duckling to the contrary and notwithstanding, the kid with the curly hair is the girl who gets the handsome prince . . . and the ugly sister gets the shaft. That's the way it always had been between Catherine Broshears and her younger sister, Susanna.

On December 6, 1832, when Catherine was married to a dashing riverboat captain named Israel Broshears, the family put together a "grand" wedding for her. There were four bridesmaids and four groomsmen and a great number of guests. A grand dinner party was provided for the entire wedding party following the ceremony.

Seven years later when Susanna reached the age of sixteen years—which was considered a marriageable age in those days—the family fortunes were dissipated. There was no dashing captain and a whole bunch of suitors seeking her hand. There was only a dirt poor dirt farmer by the name of Samuel Rider. The existence or non-existence of a beautiful face meant nothing to Sam Rider. He was almost entirely sightless.

By that time, Israel Broshears had parted with his glamorous job as a riverboat captain and, along with other members of the family, he was trying to eke out a living on a farm in Pike County, Illinois.

In the meantime Susanna's adored older brother, Michael T. Simmons, had gone west to find the pot of gold at the end of the rainbow, in Oregon . . . and it looked like he had found it in a far-off place called Olympia on Puget Sound in the Oregon Territory. From the letters received at home, Mike had struck it rich. And, all of them should come out there and share his wealth.

They decided to go west.

The relative financial status of the two sisters appears in the kinds of equipment their husbands had been able to purchase for the trip west. Having disposed of his farm, Broshears bought nothing but the best, an enormous Conestoga wagon drawn by five yoke of oxen and two cows, along with a full complement of animals as a relief team. Susanna and Sam Rider had to content themselves with a lighter wagon and a pair of oxen, with some additional back-up animals. All of Catherine's equipment was of the newest and best. Susanna and Sam had to be content with the castoffs of the rest of the family. Catherine was thirty-two, Susanna twenty-five years old.

Hopefully, they were headed for a new and happy life.

But one thing hadn't changed. Catherine was the rich and beautiful sister. Susanna was the poor relation.

Damsel in distress

The Broshears-Morton-Rider wagon train left Illinois in December, 1850, and headed for Missouri where the wagon trains departed. They left March 22, intending to go slow and take plenty of time . . . During the latter part of the first week in June, Israel Broshears was taken with cholera and after him six members of their party.

with fatal results. (Twice as many as that in the train contracted the disease but survived.)

"A stream of rapidly moving immigrants passed by. 'Hurry on!' they shouted. 'Leave the dead! Save yourselves! You'll die if you stop to bury them! Help you? No!' Past the plague spot they went, in abject terror, whipping their animals to hasten their movements to the utmost." (That was Catherine's memory.)

Then a miracle happened.

The messenger who had been sent for help emerged from the mists.

Behind him was a powerfully built man wearing a wide-brimmed hat which dripped rain to a long black cape. He was riding a mule.

"This man's a doctor," the messenger said.

Catherine's narrative continued with: "He was . . . taken first to Mrs. Morton, who was then near death. 'Never mind me,' she said, 'but look after my widowed daughter, my daughter with the blind husband and the others. I am going. Help them, doctor. Don't desert my children.' "

Catherine was too ill to pay much attention to the man who had come to the aid of their stricken party . . . But Susanna had been but lightly touched by cholera. The doctor treated her with a courtesy and respect to which she was unaccustomed. He allowed her to help him with the other patients and praised her for her help.

The praise was music to her.

The doctor looked up at her with kindness and understanding when her mother begged him to take care of "my daughter with the blind husband."

The doctor became a knight in shining armor.

A number of historians have taken cognizance of Doc Maynard's efforts during that crisis with the Broshears-Morton-Rider wagon train on the plains, but none as literally as Robert Cantwell in *The Hidden Northwest*. Cantwell and his wife revisited the scene with the aid of Judge William Dietrich, president of the North Platte Historical Society, retracing the doctor's steps . . . finally producing a map which shows how it was done.

"At first glance his story seems incredible. He wrote that he had remained with the sick and dying from noon of one day, all through the night, until dawn. Then he rode forward 20 miles to catch up with the wagon train with which he had been traveling. Then he rode back 20 miles . . . or 40 miles in all, after a sleepless night. And now after joining Mrs. Broshears he rode forward with her at least another 20 miles . . . He then rode forward another 3 miles to his original wagon train to make arrangements to shift his duds to the widow's wagon the next day. Two days without sleep and more than 60 miles of hard riding were involved . . ."

Cantwell then points out that Judge Dietrich was the great authority of emigrant crossings of the Platte River. The judge showed him the various places where the river could have been crossed. He pointed out the difficulties of travel over the Oregon Trail that the emigrants accepted as a matter of course . . . "He could have done it," Judge Dietrich said . . . "It would have been hard, but he could have done it."

On June 7, with his usual brevity, Doc recorded the crisis with: "Find plenty of doctoring to do."

But by the next day, a literary transformation had overcome him. He expounded with, "Left the camp of distress on the open prairie at half past 4 in the morning. The widow was ill in both body and mind. I gave them slight encouragement by promising to return and assist them along. I overtook our company at noon twenty miles away. Went back and met the others in trouble enough. I traveled with them until night. Again overtook our company three miles ahead. Made my arrangements to shift my duds to the widow's wagon when they come up in the morning . . ."

After nine long years of Lydia, who hated his guts, the doctor had discovered a beautiful damsel in distress . . .

How long can a wagon master survive in a democratic society?

Overnight, the doctor found himself wagon master of a train that probably consisted of ten wagons.

He got the job about the way an office boy might become president of a corporation overnight . . . by virtue of the fact that the president and all of the six vice presidents had died . . . leaving the office boy as the only remaining human being in the organization who understood the filing system.

Seven people in what has become known as the Broshears-Morton-Rider party died in the twenty days succeeding June 6 when Israel Broshears keeled over in his tracks. Because she was the richest survivor of the bunch, the chore of wagon mistress devolved on Catherine Broshears. But from a standpoint of muscle alone, she was far too fragile to drive a team of seven yoke of oxen. It's not exactly like getting behind the wheel of an automobile, you know. Driving seven yoke of oxen was no mean trick . . .

Driving a yoke of *two* oxen is no mean trick.

Prosch wrote: "The widow found in the beginning that the doctor (David S. Maynard) was not a first class teamster. In fact, it was his first experience with an ox team, and to put a novice in charge of seven yoke of cattle under such circumstances was imposing a burden and strain upon him of momentous character . . ."

In short, Doc became what is known as a "bull-whacker." At the time Prosch wrote his monograph, everybody in the United States knew what a bull-whacker was, but that knowledge is considerably more limited today. One General James F. Rusling, U.S. Army, retired, provided us with a fair to middling description of some professional bull-whackers in action in his book, *Across America,* published in 1874. The general wrote his book with the idea that the railroad soon would span the country and an appreciation of the role of the bull-whacker in the development of the West would be lost forever. The scene of the following was that portion of the Oregon Trail across the Blue Mountains in northeastern Oregon between the Snake River and Umatilla, an area which the doctor would reach three months later.

In his chapter on "Journeys by Wagon Through the Blue Mountains," General Rusling wrote that he had thought army muleskinners were the toughest men on earth until he encountered the bull-whacker, and continued with:

"A harder or rougher set than the ox men or bull-whackers (as they call themselves) of the Plains and Mountains, it would be difficult perhaps to find, or even imagine . . . with their many-yoked teams, struggling through the mud and rocks . . . they were in their element . . . red-shirted, big-booted, brigand-looking ruffians, with the inseparable bowie-knife and revolver tucked around their waists, they swung and cracked their great whips like fiends, and beat their poor oxen along, as if they had no faith in the law of kindness here, or belief in a place of punishment hereafter. And when they came to a really bad place—in crossing a stream or when they struck a stump or foundered in a mud-hole—it is hard to say whether their prodigious, multiplied, and many-headed oaths were more grotesque or horrible. To say 'they swore till all was blue,' would be but a feeble comparison, the whole Mountains corruscated with sulphur . . .

"At extra bad places, the teams were doubled or trebled up, and then the wagons were bound to come, if the wood and iron only held together. Twenty or thirty yoke of oxen struggling to the chains; with the 'bull-whackers' all pounding and yelling like mad, their huge whip-lashes thick as one's wrist cracking like pistols, was a sight to see— 'muscular,' indeed in all its parts. The noise and confusion, the oaths and thwacks and splashing of mud, made it indeed the very hell of animals; but, for all that, the wagon was sure to reach *terra firma* at last . . ."

Not all of the trip would be that bad, of course.

And some of it would be worse.

So there Doc stood on June 9 facing the seven yoke of oxen— fourteen animals—hooked to Catherine's covered wagon. In his hands was a bull-whip with a handle as thick as his wrist and a plaited rawhide lash twenty-five feet long at the end of it. The object was to crack that whip over and above, under and on these animals for the next 2,000 miles.

Under the amused eyes of the other members of the party, the doctor decided that for the time, at least, he would not be under the necessity of wearing his frocked coat and flowered vest.

Doc, who had been practicing the art with his previous companions, cracked the whip and the wagon lurched slowly under way. Prosch notes that Catherine had a "large strong wagon and first class equipment," which would have included about $1,500 worth of harness animals, along with three sets of harnesses . . . horses and cattle worth some $500. The oxen were capable of hauling 400 pounds apiece, permitting her to carry nearly a ton and a half. Included in the equipment were dutch ovens for stews and for baking bread, a set of kettles that fit one inside of another . . . tin plates, knives, forks, spoons and cups . . . water kegs . . . 600 pounds of flour . . . 625 pounds of bacon . . . twenty pounds of dried apples . . . seventy-five pounds of sugar . . . two bushels of dried beans and bushel of salt . . . fifty pounds of coffee and an equivalent amount of tea . . . thirty-six packets of dried yeast, two gallons of vinegar . . . saws . . . shovels . . . axes . . . and all of the hand tools which Israel Broshears had accumulated in his life as a farmer for the previous decade or so . . . along with rifles, shotguns and hand guns . . . tobacco.

Added to these were a number of family heirlooms which Catherine had been unable to part with—but which she would have to part with before the end of the journey.

The elimination of anything beyond the 2,800 pounds which the team could haul began immediately, and what with six deaths in the family, that meant a lot of discarding—including whole wagon loads.

It was pathetically typical of the conditions on the trail.

It is impossible for me to resist quoting the courtly Prosch with regard to the next period in the reincarnation of Doctor Maynard, one in which there was a lapse in Doc's journal: "Here there is a break in the doctor's journal, there being no entries from June 12 to 24th inclusive . . . it is to be supposed that the troubles were so many and the labors so great incident to the peculiar situation in which he found himself that he was unable to keep the diary written up . . . Mrs. Broshears losing not only her husband and mother but three other relatives, and being left in a most forlorn and helpless condition. The sympathy and assistance she required from the doctor, who became her second husband, accounts reasonably for this much to be regretted omission in the narrative."

Truth impels me to point out another aspect of the human condition with regard to the omissions in the doctor's diary. The chances are that as a precautionary measure, anyone displaying any symptoms of cholera got the full treatment from the doctor on the grounds that it was a lot better to be safe than sorry. So the calomel was passed out with careless abandon. The purgative treatment was followed by the accepted dosages of an opium based tonic to sooth the irritated linings of the collective intestines in the party . . .

Leaving everybody in a happy state of euphoria.

At the end of two weeks—with only Austin Morton hovering between life and death—the folks sobered up some and realized there had been no new cases of cholera in the group . . . enabling them to look at the doctor more as man than magician . . .

And when he cut off the supply of opium, with considerably less than outright enthusiasm.

There's nothing like knowing your business for gaining the respect of the people who are supposed to be your followers, and the doctor was in a tough spot for wagon master when he didn't have a "real" grasp on the fine art of driving oxen . . . a feat in which men half his age on the wagon train could perform better. He adopted the obnoxious policy of requiring that potholes be dug in the banks of the river for filtered drinking water. Unlike the river water which was jovially described as too thin to farm and too thick to drink, it came clear. But it had the awful taste of alkali. The river water came out like cocoa and frequently had tadpoles swimming in the bottom of the cup, but it tasted good. He insisted that it be filtered and boiled, a tedious and annoying process.

Moreover, he was stuffed with "book larnin'." The kind of expertise that the doctor picked up in his preparations for the transcontinental journey was that offered by Peter Burnett who had organized one of the first emigrant trains to cross the Oregon Trail eight years earlier. Appearing in national magazines to which most of the party did not have access, this kind of advice cautioned would-be travelers to take care of their animals early on so the animals could take care of them when the going got rough later on. Without the oxen, mules and horses, they wouldn't get across the Rockies. Burnett wrote. "They should be regularly watered, morning, noon and night. Never maltreat them, but govern them as you would a woman, with kindness, affection and caresses, and you will be rewarded by their docility . . . The best way to save the teams is to drive a reasonable distance every day and stop about an hour before sundown. This gives time for arranging the camp, and for the teams to rest and eat before it is dark. Eight hours' drive in long days—resting one hour at noon—I think is enough. Never drive irregularly if you can avoid it. A prudent care should be taken of horses, teams, and provisions from the start . . ."

The doctor added his own fillip to these instructions.

And that's where he broke his pick.

His insistence on cleanliness was quite a time-consumer, but one they obliged him with as long as there was sickness in the party. But now he was proposing that once a week, when they came to a good watering spot, they not only do their collective laundry, but take baths.

Laundry? Baths!

Too much!

For people driving desperately to leave the source of the dread cholera, this was one delay too many. The first inkling of his dethronement came on the morning of June 25th, just two weeks after he had been voted into power. He wrote in his journal: "Started late, in consequence of our cattle being lost. When I came up from hunting the cattle the company had gone and left us. We drove on to the Bad Hills, about eighteen miles." (Where they caught up with the others and encamped.)

The next day, they buried Austin Morton, in what was his last act as wagon master. They only made two miles that day, and the doctor found himself getting the silent treatment. Nobody would talk to him.

The man and the animals

The campground that night was on the banks of the river where they encountered a disconsolate young man by the name of George Benton. George Benton was in tough shape, as Prosch explains:

"George Benton, a nephew of Senator Thomas H. Benton, had started with another party which met with disaster in the river South Platte. Several wagons and animals were lost at a supposed ford, where the water was both deep and strong. Benton saved his life and his horse, but lost all else, including shoes, coat and hat, and being left entirely alone on one side of the river. He, perhaps, saved the Broshears-Morton people a similar misfortune by pointing out the danger, and he immediately took service with them at $18 per month and clothes, the latter being an advance payment that was absolutely necessary . . ."

Doc's sole comment on the incident was made the next day. It read: "George Benton commenced driving the team."

The big confrontation with the others came on June 27—eighteen days after the doctor had taken over and one day after George Benton had signed on. The party reached Cottonwood Creek. There was excellent feed, fuel and water. The doctor-cum-wagon master announced they would stay here for the next couple of days, do a laundry, bathe themselves and rest the teams.

There were angry mutterings from the others on the train.

Laundry . . .

Rest the teams . . .

Take baths!

No way!

"You can stay if you want," the doctor was told. "The rest of us are leaving."

Samuel Rider, virtually sightless, had no choice. He would be required to go with the others or not continue on the trip.

And that's when Susanna stood up in the doctor's defense. With shining eyes, she announced that she would drive their team if necessary. "We will stay with Doctor Maynard," she announced. It was partly because the doctor had waded for wood for the Riders and had shown them the same kinds of little courtesies that he accorded anyone else who ever needed his help. The little kindnesses were common to the doctor . . . But not to Susanna. She took them as a personal tribute to herself.

The doctor wrote: "Part with Fanings & Co."

The record doesn't show how many wagons there were when the rest of the members of the party voted "Fanings" in as the new wagon master. I'm guessing eight or ten . . . at least the majority of the group . . . leaving the doctor as master of two wagons, Catherine's and her sister Susanna's. George Benton had appeared at a particularly propitious time. Susanna's blind husband was in no position to drive the Rider's oxen, while the doctor, who had mastered the art by this time, could take on the smaller wagon with one yoke of animals.

On June 28, the members of Doc's diminished group did a laundry and bathed. The doctor packed a picnic lunch and he and Catherine and Susanna took their horses on a hunting trip. It was a beautiful day. The flowers were blooming. And the new regime began with pleasure on the part of everybody concerned. That night, the doctor wrote: "I think this is the pleasantest hunting ground I ever saw." That night there was fresh game for dinner for the people involved. That night, as they sat around their bright campfire, the world was pleasant indeed.

The next day, they crossed from the South Platte to the North Platte, where we get another sample of the doctor's free and easy approach to the spending of money. What most travelers described as "those thieving Indians" had established a ferry at the most favorable spot to cross the river. You either paid to cross there or took a drive some-place else where the river could be forded. The doctor cheerfully paid.

Israel Broshears and Samuel Rider had followed the general practice of the time and had brought along as many extra animals as they could afford to buy—as sort of "spares" for hauling the wagons . . . and as an investment. For the most part, they brought along extra cattle. The cows could be milked, providing a welcome additon to the often dubious water on the trail, as well as in the cooking. And, as one writer of the time pointed out, the animals which could be trans-ported to Oregon would be worth "thribble as much as when you started." Another wrote that "If a man had $500 and would invest it in young heifers in the States and drive them here (to Oregon), they would be worth $5,000; and by engaging in stock raising, he could make an independent fortune. Milch cows on the road are exceedingly useful, as they give an abundance of milk all the way . . ."

It wasn't all that easy, of course. The loose animals fell behind those harnessed to the wagons. They also ate all of the grass that otherwise would have been found on either side of the trail. "Trail" is really kind of a loose term. Depending upon the particular conditions at any given time, it could be as much as 100 miles wide. It's been estimated there must have been 100,000 animals crossing the trail every summer. Thus the drovers connected with the wagon trains often strayed far and wide.

And the situation gives us further insight into the kind of a man Doc Maynard was. He took on as his own responsibility the business of scouting ahead for wood, water and feed—with especial emphasis on the latter. If he didn't take care of the animals, they couldn't take care of him. On a good day, the wagons would make twenty miles. The doctor, ranging far and wide, covered twice that amount of ground. Then at night, when the rest of the party collapsed, he took the evening meal to the drovers, wherever they were. There were many notations like the following in his journal: "Had a serious tramp in carrying supper to the boys, after dark, some six or seven miles and back."

How many men of forty-two could ride a horse for forty miles a day, collect the wood and water necessary to make camp, and then tramp twelve to fourteen miles on foot in the dark without the aid of a flashlight? No wonder there were the frequent entries in his diary reading, "went to bed at midnight, (or two o'clock in the morning) . . . tired enough."

"Tired enough," with or without an exclamation point that was the signal that Maynard had reached total exhaustion. Total exasperation was expressed with such expressions as, "oh God, the mosquitoes," and "if they don't beat the devil." But most of the time his strongest editorial comment was the one used when he encountered the Broshears wagon train: "In trouble enough."

Shakespeare, he was not.

The doctor worked for the animals "hard enough."

Some samples of his entries go like this: "The team came in full and lively," or the "team was rested and recruited."

There were other entries, though, like, "feed poor . . . camped without feed or water . . . found plenty of salertus water, by which our teams suffered much . . ." On the third of July, they found no feed. On the fourth, he reported that they "celebrated a little." Other times it was, "found feed very scarce . . . dragged team through sand eight miles to devil's Gate . . . Oxen sick, vomiting like dogs. Old Nig looks bad, got better towards night . . . team comfortably fed . . . team tolerably fed but no water . . ."

Here's as good a sample as any. "July 15—Left camp and passed the forks of the roads, the left road leading to Salt Lake. Traveled eight miles to the Little Sandy. Watered the team, drove three miles more, turned out and camped. Drove the team up four miles further for feed. Set things right about camp, carried supper to the boys four miles, washed, changed clothes and slept in tent . . ."

No guard duty?

A red letter day!

On other days he wrote, "found good feed for team four and a half miles from camp, and stayed to rest our teams in the waters of the Little Sandy . . . went in search of feed; tramped eleven miles and found feed scarce. Returned to camp and sent the boys out with the teams to graze all night . . . Lion and Bright are sick . . . we threw Lion down and found four or five gravel stones in his foot. Came eighteen miles and camped with most excellent water and feed . . ."

The doctor cared for the animals . . .

And the animals took care of him.

The cattle had given him everything they had. "Lion, Sam and Bright are sick," he wrote that night. For several days after that there was excellent feed and water, but the animals were in trouble . . . and he delayed the trip to nurse them, writing, "Doctored Lion's foot and fed poor Bright."

Things began to go bad for Lion and the doctor took him out of the harness. On July 31, he found the mosquitoes too bad for either the people or the animals and they had to move on. August 1, the doctor was sick himself and under the influence of calomel pills, but he drove the animals "eight miles through the sage to a spring, and put old Lion out to rest." The next day he reported, "Started late on Lion's account. Drove two-and-a-half miles and he gave up the ghost . . ."

When they reached the end of the trail, an effort was made to guide them over Naches Pass in the Cascade Mountains, but the doctor opined the animals had given their all . . . could never make it over the pass. They had earned a rest. He could have gotten a handsome price for them, but he sold them for a mere $110 in order to get them a good home.

Doc figured they'd earned it.

That's the way he did things.

Particularly today, when we don't have that much contact with them, people may think it odd that a man could have deep affection for oxen and have that feeling reciprocated. But the doctor did. Those patient, dumb beasts had been his close companions for weary months on the trail. They had done his bidding and had never failed him. They had bivouacked together, slept together, lunched together. They knew him and were eager to obey him. Without them the journey would not have been possible.

It was with sadness that he parted with them.

The doctor's system had worked and in the long haul had passed the people like Fanings & Co. who were stalled by the side of the road, their weary animals at a point of exhaustion.

Ezra Meeker also had a cogent word or two on the subject:

"With so many, the watchword was to push ahead and make as big a day's drive as possible." Of a thousand wagons that crossed the original river with Meeker's group, soon all were ahead of them. He quoted his wagon master as saying, " 'Now, fellers, jist let 'em rush on, and keep cool, we'll overcatch them afore long.' And we did, and passed many a broken-down team, the result of that first few days of rush . . ."

It was a philosophy followed by Doc Maynard.

The man and the Indians

Doc had a great natural curiosity about anything that came down the main street of his life, and he satisfied it with the zest of a gourmet. His diary is peppered with examples of a mouth-breathing amazement at such things as his first sight of a fellow who would be normal in any professional basketball game today. Entered in his journal on April 21, "Saw James Porter, the Kentucky giant, 7⅔ feet." Another in a long series of entries on the natural beauties of the country through which he was traveling west goes: "This pass through the Whitewater is one of the curiosities of nature. Perpendicular height of rocks four hundred feet. Width of stream or valley fifty-five feet." On August 1, there's another sample. Sick all day and on calomel, and driven wild by the mosquitoes, he nonetheless took time off at Fort Hall to take in another human phenomenon. I haven't the slightest idea who it was, but he devoted a precious line or two in his diary to note, "Took in George the Second at the Fort."

He probably picked up the basics of Indian dialect before he ever left Cleveland, and with his facile mind was able to acquire competence in communication with them in their own language as he went along. It is certain that by the time he arrived in the Pacific Northwest, he could converse freely with them—even on abstract subjects. It was a competence that few other whites bothered with and it amazed and delighted the aboriginal residents of this country. To him, they were children, sometimes very dangerous children—children with their backs to the wall against the onslaught of the white civilization.

And he never feared them . . .

It was a condition which seemed to put a magical protection around him.

In this, he was an exception to the rule.

Most of the immigrants to Oregon were scared to death, not only of the Indians, but of the other strangers they met on the trail. Nearly all of the immigrants to Oregon Territory were simple folk who had lived a simple life in a small community before they headed west. And, most of the time, the people headed for California were the sophisticates . . . the traders, gamblers, con men and wealthy adventurers.

Doc was neither.

And he led a charmed life.

Parkman, who lived among the Indians, provides us with at least a partial answer. He wrote: "The timorous mood of the emigrants was doubly unfortunate, as it exposed them to real danger. Assume, in the presence of Indians a bold bearing, self-confident yet vigilant, and you will find them tolerably safe neighbors. But your safety depends on the respect and fear you are able to inspire. If you betray timidity or indecision, you convert them from that moment into insidious and dangerous enemies."

The Indians, and the Mormons, and anybody else who happened to be strategically-located, erected toll bridges and toll ferries at places where your choice was one of going five or ten miles up or downstream or of waiting several days for swollen rivers to subside. Following natural laws of economics, the farther west the immigrants got, the higher the tolls. The doctor's first encounter with an Indian toll ferry came on May 19, in Missouri, while he still was with the original party heading for California. The toll was twenty-five cents a wagon. By the time he got to the Snake River in Idaho, it had been upped to $7.50. This time they swam the cattle across.

On one of the more notable occasions, the doctor was called in by the chief of an Indian village to treat the chief's daughter. As was his usual custom, he visited the Indians in their villages, breaking bread with them, trading with them, and companionably smoking the inevitable peace pipe with them.

On July 28, he noted in his journal that he left camp at 7 o'clock in the morning, traveling leisurely through good roads where there was plenty of fuel, feed and water. The day before, he reported that he and Catherine had passed beautiful springs and that there were

"Indians aplenty." That day he noted that the hot springs were a curiosity. They were sulphur and soda springs and they paused for a time to admire them. Then they went on for about a mile where they paused to satisfy the curiosity of the natives in an Indian village. Catherine's tendency to fear the aboriginals was dissipated when she saw their attitude toward the doctor. On both sides, it was one of easy familiarity. She and the doctor were royally entertained with feasts in half-a-dozen tents, as was the ritual. He sold the Indians five pounds of tobacco for $2.50. And when they finally went on, they were directed to another Indian camp at an interesting location seven miles away . . . which was where they camped for the night.

The doctor covers all of this in his journal with: "Fed forenoon at an Indian camp . . . Sold five pounds of tobacco for $2.50. Went on seven miles and camped near an Indian camp." He also adds a cursory, "Was called to see a sick papoose . . ."

A crying baby is a crying baby, regardless of race, creed or color. And whatever medicine Doctor Maynard had, it was better than that of the Indians, and probably contained just a touch of opium. He had a salve compounded of mercury that, for instance, could provide real relief for the child.

And a grateful mother is a grateful mother in any language.

Catherine was impressed.

In the blindness of their attraction to one another, neither Catherine nor the doctor noticed that somebody else in their group also was impressed. Catherine's sister, Susanna.

Both women were even more impressed on the occasion of an approach by a band of hostiles on July 8. With his usual brevity, the doctor recorded the event: "Started out, and after traveling six miles discovered a party of Indians coming upon us. We heard they had just robbed one train. Prepared for an attack. When within half a mile they sent two of their number to see how strong we were. After viewing us carefully they left us for good. Traveled twenty-two miles . . ."

I could shoot Maynard, myself, for his casual dismissal of this confrontation. How did he do it? What did he say? Was he scared? Did he "con" 'em out of it? Would he have killed them if he had the chance?

Man, this was a page one story in the books written by the immigrants who wrote books.

There are dozens of examples of people on wagon trains who lost their lives in a confrontation like this one. But I suppose it comes in the same category as the fatal traffic accident that is missed by inches. You just drive on. The best Catherine came up with later on was that the doctor was "absolutely fearless when it came to Indians."

For one thing, he could discourse with them in their own language. The strength of his personality showed through to them. He was armed. He probably saw to it that everybody else in the train had guns pointed at the Indians. But there were only four people.

It was some feat.

Doc Maynard was a complex man with insights which none of us ever will fully understand. And he instinctively understood another thing about the Indians which we, with all of our so-called advantages, have not as yet fully grasped. It is something which influenced his attitude toward Indians for the rest of his life.

He sensed the reverence with which the western Indians regarded the salmon, which had been the principal source of protein in their culture for perhaps 5,000 years . . . and the feeling came to him first on August 12, 1850, when he bought one of these beautiful animals from some Indians at Salmon Falls on the Snake River. His entire association with the incident was one of beauty. He wrote, "This place is delightful. The stream is alive with fish of first quality, and wild geese are as tame as the natives." A few days later, he would write, "We killed a noble salmon, taking breakfast out of him, and a fine dish he was. I just wish my family had such a fish to work on."

Salmon was of critical importance to the doctor from then on. He knew that somewhere, somehow, it should be made available to people everywhere. It was a major consideration in the selection of the site for the city of Seattle. The technique of canning it had not as yet been developed, but the doctor sensed its importance . . .

And, as was so often the case, he was ahead of his time.

The Indians also were responsible for a major break-through in his relationship with Catherine. He traded a brass kettle, two blankets, a shirt, a mare and a colt . . .

For a "beautiful beaded Indian dress for Catherine."

It was a big day in the lives of this man and this woman.

An awful day in the life of Susanna Rider.

The man and the woman

There aren't many of us whose lives are visited by the high drama that was so much a part of the bond of unity between David and Catherine that it was commonplace to them. In later years, when he was ill, she had to take care of him. But for the better part of their lives together, he was fiercely protective of her. They developed a love which defied what normally were the irresistible mores of the day.

And the shape and direction of Washington history evolved from it.

Quite a story.

Her epitaph for the doctor was: "There was no better man on earth."

By all standards she was a beautiful woman and a relatively young one when he died. She lived on for thirty-three years, and never found a man who could replace him in her heart.

The doctor's first encounter with her came at a time when everyone in her party and all of the other immigrants around them passed the stricken wagon and demanded that the bodies of the dead be left exposed to the elements. Catherine was distraught and half-sick, and it was one of those times when the temptation to flight was close to irresistible. She couldn't dig the graves of six people all by herself. But, "Mrs. Broshears would not go until her husband, her mother and the others were buried by the roadside, their bodies as safe as they could be made from the teeth of the wolves and the scalping knives of the Indians."

It took all night . . .

But the doctor seized a shovel and helped the woman bury her dead.

There was much for Catherine to admire about the man who would become her husband. His awkwardness in handling seven yoke of oxen was immediately apparent, but he stuck at it and within two weeks could bull-whack the oxen with the best of them. His compassion for man and beast was apparent throughout the three months that they were on the trail. His good cheer was unflagging, and he brought humor into her life—something that previously had been completely lacking. There was no chore too large or too small for him to tackle. He provided her with small, thoughtful niceties that hitherto had been lacking in the man to whom she had been married.

One of the far-reaching impacts he made upon her came during the first week in July. On July fifth, the doctor literally put his shoulder to the wheel of the covered wagon as the oxen floundered through eight miles of desert sand. That night, he drove the animals out three miles to feed. The heat was intense. The next day, he brought the team back, hitched up the wagon and drove back to the spot where he had spent the night with the animals. What an iron man! He had worked for twenty hours straight, without any rest.

The water in the keg tasted of alkali . . .

And was almost too hot to drink.

Catherine dreamed of a drink of cold water.

What neither she nor the doctor realized was that somebody else also was dreaming of a drink of cold water—Susanna.

That day the doctor announced that he would be gone from camp on some mysterious errand. He carried a huge bucket with him. When he covered the subject the next morning in his journal, he noted that he had gone on a trip to a mountain and had returned with a load of fresh snow. "Got into camp about three o'clock." he wrote. "Tired enough."

But Catherine had her drink of cold water . . . so did Susanna.

She looked thoughtfully at this man . . . so did Susanna.

He had saved most of the members of her party from cholera. He had taken command of the party and of her future. He had refused to budge when the others panicked and fled the cholera. "Let them go," he said, "make haste slowly." He had taken her with him to treat the sick Indian papoose. He had out-bluffed a band of hostile Indians. He had exercised calm, cool judgment in every situation to which he had been exposed. He was a tower of strength accompanied by a gentleness that she never had seen in a man.

One of the chores the doctor assumed for himself was that of guard duty at night . . . against the Indians . . . against the Mormons . . . against stampeding buffalo. The various Indian tribes were warring more on one another on the trail than against the emigrants. But what they needed most was horses . . . and their nightly raids were made more for these animals than for any other reason.

During the day, the doctor scouted ahead for fuel, feed and water. Ezra Meeker described the situation: "The grass along the beaten track was always eaten off close by loose stock . . . so we had frequently to take the cattle long distances from camp. Then came the most trying part of the whole trip—the all night watch, which resulted in our making the cattle our bedfellows, back to back for warmth; for signal as well, to get up if the ox did. It was not long, though, till we were used to it, and slept quite a bit except when a storm struck; well, then, to say the least, it was not a pleasure outing.

"But weren't we glad when the morning came, with, perchance, the smoke of the campfire in sight, and maybe, as we approached, we could catch the aroma of the coffee; and then such tender greetings and such thoughtful care that would have touched a heart of stone, and to us seemed like paradise. We were supremely happy."

Meeker was a young man at the time . . . talking about his young wife. But the emotional climate was identical for the lonesome, bereaved widow and for the man who had been living in an atmosphere of hate for nine long years.

The spirit might be willing for morality.

But the flesh is something else again.

And that didn't just apply to Catherine.

It also applied to Susanna. And the part of the marriage ceremony that reads "till death do us part" is honored as much in the breach as not. The law says you have to be married to this woman or this man

. . . but it doesn't necessarily hold that you have to remain in love with him. And a complicating factor had entered into the idyllic picture.

Susanna had fallen in love with the handsome doctor.

On July 11, Susanna found her sister in the doctor's arms.

In the resulting shock waves that hit Susanna, her love for the doctor turned to hate.

Trouble in paradise

Trouble appeared in paradise the very next day. It was fifteen days since the doctor's cursory notation. "Parted with Fanings & Co." This time he wrote: "Left Sweetwater and traveled over the ragged mountains twenty miles. I was well worn out, as well as the team, from watching all night. A miserable company for help."

They were at the Continental Divide.

Things did not improve the following day.

After noting that the team had been poorly fed the night before, he added: "Traveled eight miles to the last of the Sweetwater and turned out with a view to stopping, but the company growled, and we set sail. Went in search of food and water until all power exhausted. Team got ahead about five miles. Camped with little feed and no water."

On the fourteenth, they covered a bare eight miles again and the other members of the party waited disconsolately while the doctor went in search of feed and water. He wrote, "Found some feed but no water. Got no thanks from the company for my labor."

The going was tough at this point. The whole party—two wagons and the various animals connected with them—averaged about twelve miles a day when it hoped to average around twenty. But the doctor, foraging ahead for feed and water and then walking four to six miles each night after they had stopped for the day to take "supper to the boys" was covering thirty-two to thirty-six miles a day, either in the saddle or on foot.

Then he stood guard at night about half the time.

The animals and the people all traveled about half as far as he did and got twice as much rest.

On July sixteenth, after traveling four and a half miles, they found good feed and water and, as wagon master, he called a halt for the rest of the day . . . and would have stayed there the next day but "the company growled so much I consented to start next morning." The next day, they covered twelve miles and he covered an additional eleven miles looking for feed and water.

The eighteenth was a terrible day.

After filling every container with water, they left camp at eleven o'clock in the morning. They were crossing a desert where "dust from one to twelve inches deep on the ground and above the top of the wagon cover a perfect cloud." They traveled all day and all night . . . crossing twelve miles of plain and then "went over a tremendous mountain."

Tension perceptibly increased.

The doctor tried to "rest and recruit" the animals.

The Riders insisted on pressing ahead, regardless of what it did to the animals.

On July twenty-first, the doctor wrote: "Company was not willing to feed the team or for me to doctor Lion. We therefore started without even watering the team. Came on about four miles and camp."

The next day the split came.

The Riders fell back and the doctor went back to find out what was wrong and learned that their animals were too weak to travel. Harsh words were exchanged. The doctor and Catherine went on for fifteen miles that day. The trail was easy and they could have gone farther, but they were stopped by a violent rainstorm . . . enabling the Riders to catch up with them. The Riders "camped in sight" but not with the doctor and Catherine. Doc Maynard stalked over and got his tent from them.

The last time they saw the Riders on the Oregon Trail was on July

27 when the doctor reported that he saw them "some three miles astern."

On August third, they reached the next important fork in the road of the doctor's life. It was at the confluence of the Snake and the Raft rivers . . .

The last chance to head for California.

Could he leave Catherine alone on the trail?

No way!

George Benton announced that he would leave them there and head for California. "In a pig's eye!" the doctor retorted.

Well, not precisely like that.

The doctor covered it in his diary with: "In quite a hubbub. George is about to leave us for California." The doctor's words on the subject were mild, but the young man got the point.

George didn't leave.

He continued on with them.

For the next sixty days—and *nights*—the doctor and Catherine were alone and unchaperoned on the Oregon Trail . . .

And for the next sixty days—and *nights*—the scorned Susanna followed in their tracks . . . falling farther behind as the days passed . . . burning her cork with increasing intensity every day . . .

Vividly imagining what the doctor and her sister were doing.

On September twenty-fifth, the doctor wrote: "Made our way . . . to M. T. Simmons, our place of destination, where we were received with a degree of brotherly kindness which seemed to rest our weary limbs, and promise of asylum for us in our worn-out pilgrimage."

Oh! Susanna

I can tell you for cotton pickin', boll weevil, gin mill certain that Stephen Collins Foster didn't have *our* Susanna in mind when he wrote the song about the girl with the same name for people to sing around the campfire at night on the Oregon Trail . . . and in the local saloons when they got to Oregon or California.

I also can vouch for the fact that her name has never appeared in many Seattle history books. For that matter, she has barely made it in *any* history book to date.

But, oh, boy, what a wallop she packed in Northwest history.

In order to understand her impact, it is necessary to go back a ways into the Simmons family history which, as far as Catherine was concerned began with her maternal grandfather, Michael Troutman. Michael was married twice . . . had ten children by each wife. He was worth plenty of bucks. At a family gathering for Christmas two years before Catherine was born, there were ten of his children there . . . ninety grandchildren and three great grandchildren. "All of the 122 sat down to dinner in the dining room, the length of which was eighty feet, the house being a three-story brick as large as a European castle . . ."

The landed possessions of the Troutman family included some 30,000 acres.

And, alongside the Simmons family, they were *poverty stricken!*

The Simmons family had three plantations, one for cotton, one for hemp and one for corn . . . and 300 slaves to operate the whole shebang.

When a Troutman and a Simmons were married, it resembled a merger between General Motors and the little company put together by Henry Ford.

But the war of 1812 and a few other similar disasters did in the family wealth. By the time one of the major characters of Washington history, Michael Troutman Simmons had reached young manhood, they were broke.

But they never forgot the "glory days."

Historian Hubert Bancroft describes Simmons as a fine specimen of a man "possessing the fine physique of the early men of Kentucky,

unlettered though not unenlightened, he possessed the qualities which in feudal times made men chiefs and founders of families. His courage was only exceeded by his independence . . ." Mike was seventeen years old and approaching his maximum growth of six feet four inches when his father died and he left the family farm to make his own way.

On January 1, 1835, he married Elizabeth Kindred. Mike was twenty years old. Elizabeth was sixteen.

Mike and Elizabeth moved to Missouri where, "Mike struggled with a text on mathematics. By rule of 'cut fir,' he constructed an excellent grist mill . . . not far from what became the site of St. Joseph. He was known the country over as 'honest Mike' Simmons. His mill was the meeting place for all the countryside where all problems large and small, were discussed . . ."

In the winter of 1843-44, Mike sold his mill and became a colonel in a huge wagon train of 300 wagons headed for Oregon. He had intended to settle in the Rogue River country, but when the train reached Fort Vancouver, he learned that the Hudson's Bay Company, under the autocratic management of Dr. John McLoughlin, was *requiring* all American settlers to take up claims south of the Columbia. The idea of the British at that time was that the Columbia

River would be the boundary between the United States and Canada. And when Mike learned the British wouldn't let him go north, then that is exactly what he had to do. Mike was a man who was easily led—but he couldn't be driven.

In July of 1845, Mike explored Puget Sound as far north as Whidbey Island, but finally staked a claim at the head of Budd Inlet where the Deschutes River dropped eighty feet in a series of falls and was an admirable spot for another grist mill. The mill went into operation in 1846, and was the first on Puget Sound. The following year, he erected a hydraulically operated sawmill—another first on the Sound—in what became the town of Tumwater.

In the fall of 1849, Mike sold his mills to Clanrick Crosby (Bing's grandfather) for $35,000. He was offered free property by Edmund Sylvester, the town proprietor, on the main street if he would come two miles north to the town of Olympia and establish there the first general store owned by an American on Puget Sound. If you will remember to multiply by ten to get the $35,000 in perspective, you will get some notion of the impact Mike's financial condition had on the rest of his impoverished family, which by that time was struggling for an existence in Illinois.

Early in 1850, Mike took a small portion of his fortune and purchased controlling interest in the brig *Orbit,* the first merchant vessel to visit the Sound . . . sent it to San Francisco with a load of pilings and an order for the ingredients of his new store. He erected a two-story building at the corner of First Avenue and Main Street. It became the first American store and postoffice on Puget Sound . . . and Mike, the first merchant and postmaster.

Overnight, Mike was the richest and most influential American on the Sound.

And that's what he was when Catherine and the doctor showed up in Olympia.

They told Mike the story of their suffering and struggle . . . of the deep and turbulent rivers . . . the precipitous mountains and the burning deserts . . . the worry about the animals and the vehicles . . . the sickness and the disease . . . the encounter with the Indians and the fear of the Mormons . . . and some kind of a cockimamy story about the separation from Susanna and Sam Rider.

Catherine got into the touchy ground about the death of her husband and the sixty days and sixty nights she and the doctor had spent unchaperoned on the trail.

In those days, *one* night alone wth a man was ruinous to a woman's reputation.

She admitted that it was a little soon after the death of Israel. On the other hand, this was the age of enlightenment. She and Israel had not been getting on that well in the previous few years. After all she was only sixteen when she and Israel had been married. She still was a young woman, etc., etc.

And they were going to be married.

Mike was something of a man of the world, himself, and could understand the story so far. He had his private suspicions of the doctor even at that point. It has been a long time, for instance, since anybody in the Simmons, Troutman, Morton or Broshears family had been in silks and satins. And here was this guy who *said* he was a doctor . . .

A lot of men *said* they were doctors.

Maynard, who had gotten himself barbered and shaved for the negotiations with Mike, stood there with his string tie and flowered vest, his polished black boots and expensive suit . . . his clean fingernails, white shirt and expensive cufflinks.

Catherine was wearing the Indian Maiden costume the doctor had bought her at great expense near Walla Walla.

Mike was more or less going along with the gag when they dropped the bombshell on him.

"There's this one small difficulty."

"Ah?"

"The doctor already has a wife."

"Holy smoke!"

Well, she knew that when he left, he had left for good. She did not expect him back. She had agreed to get a divorce on grounds of desertion as soon as the legal time had elapsed. However, in view of this new, er, "development," the doctor would arrange to get an immediate divorce. Prosch worded it like this: "He would treat Mrs. Broshears honorably, would marry with her, and in the most correct manner would end the trouble."

Left to his own devices, Mike might have gone along with them. Then, ten days later, Susanna showed up with murder in her head, blood in her eye and a loaded gun in her hands.

The Simmons family histories have been a little diffident about this episode in the family history. As one of the family historians pointed out, nothing ever was said about the "scandal of Catherine and Doctor Maynard."

Catherine pointed out that her brother was a head taller than the doctor, and with considerable pride told her biographer that Susanna tried to kill the doctor but that the "latter was not intimidated, nor more by white men and women than by Indians or disease."

Memory of the phantom lady mocked Maynard . . .

And this time he would not give up so easily.

III

For Love . . .
or Money?

Doc Maynard, who appears to be a mild-mannered man in most instances, could be a rough cob when occasion dictated. For instance, he didn't hit the roof and blow somebody's head off when he found his first wife in bed with another man. What he did was set a course for himself that took nine tough years to achieve results. With no big fanfare, he just plugged away at it; probably driving his first wife right out of her tree in the process . . . but never stopping until he attained his goal.

The doctor was not a huge man, but when necessity demanded that he become a mule-whacker with a twenty-five-foot whip, he flailed away until he got the hang of it and then come hell or high water, he drove that team of oxen across the country. The Indians who approached him on the trail with malice aforethought, didn't find him breathing fire and brimstone, but they got the message just the same. He didn't holler and stir up a storm when an insanely jealous Susanna presented him with the business end of a gun. But she got the message from a pair of steady eyes and didn't pull the trigger.

In the next few months, the doctor would face down and tame a shrewd, cruel and uniquely amoral Indian chief. He determined that Catherine would become his wife and went about accomplishing that result in spite of all the roadblocks her family put in his path.

At the end of this period of his life he liberated what would become downtown Seattle from the custody of a naive young man from Cherry Grove, Illinois, as easily as though he were removing a surface splinter from a man's hand. And then, within a matter of hours, he named and started the City of Seattle.

The honeymoon ended on October 7, 1850, when Susanna tried to kill him . . . and the wedding bells had not as yet rung.

By that time, the doctor realized that California was out as far as he was concerned. All they had down there was gold. What there was in the Pacific Northwest was without a doubt the greatest challenge of his life. For thirty years now, there had been a movement to link the Atlantic and Pacific coasts with some kind of a road.

We think that with all the airplanes flying around we've got a better handle on things than the folks did back in those days . . . but they were as aware of the Great Circle Route across the Pacific then as we are today.

Cognizant of all of this, the legislators of the two-year-old Oregon Territory were regularly sending off resolutions to Congress demanding that we get protection for our waters against the British . . . demanding that Alaska be made a territory . . . demanding that coastal defenses, lighthouses and harbors be mapped and charted . . . demanding that a telegraph line be extended to the new territory.

And demanding a transcontinental railroad.

The rage for laying out towns was at its height.

Some town in the Oregon Territory was going to become the "Queen City of the Pacific Northwest" and the "Gateway to the riches of the Orient" via the Great Circle Route. And at least twenty-five promoters of twenty-five towns during that two-year period had entered the sweepstakes.

If a fella could make his town the terminus of the railroad, he could sit back and make a fortune.

Doc Maynard was the ultimate gambler.

At fifty cents a call, there wasn't enough money in doctoring . . . So, what he did was decide to enter the incorporational sweepstakes.

He'd had a lot more experience in city-building than the average promoter in the Pacific Northwest at the time . . . and this kind of thing would keep him close to Catherine . . .

So, why not give it a fling?

Chance is the golden opportunity of the trained mind

Detective stories tell about how the police department, with all their anti-crime equipment and know-how, have caught the criminal. What usually happens is they dust for fingerprints, interview the neighbors, question the relatives and all like that.

Then some stool pigeon calls up and tells them who done it—and where he or she is at that moment.

And that's how the doctor located the site on which Seattle was built. He could have pored over the reports of Commander Charles Wilkes, who had explored the whole Pacific Coast nine years earlier. And he could have talked to all the experts about the best possible location for a city, etc., but what he did was pick up the *Oregon Spectator* for October 17, 1850 . . .

And there it was . . .

Cleveland West laid out before his very eyes.

Another man with a bright mind and a lively curiosity had arrived in Olympia nine months earlier in search of a place to settle.

The man was Isaac N. Ebey.

Mike Simmons, the only merchant in the place—which was called Smithfield at the time—tried to interest Ebey in settling down in his candidate for "Queen City" and "Gateway to the Orient." And Ebey did plunk up for a couple of town lots. But it didn't look like a very hot spot to him. Beyond suggesting that they change the name from Smithfield to Olympia, he didn't play much of a role in the place.

Ebey wasn't even sure he wanted to promote a town.

What he did want to do was explore Puget Sound. He agreed that he would inform Mike about his progress. And in the summer of 1850 he wrote a letter to Mike extolling the virtues of a place on what then was called Duwamish Bay and now is known as Elliott Bay.

Mike, who figured himself as some kind of an empire builder, forwarded Ebey's letter to the *Oregon Spectator* in the hope that it would encourage more settlers to head north of the Columbia.

The paper ran the letter two days after the doctor showed up in town in search of a divorce.

Maybe it was Mike's name on the letter which caught the doctor's eye. But Maynard was a man of infinite curiosity, and he probably would have read the piece under any circumstances.

Whatever it was, the seed that grew into the city of Seattle was planted in Maynard's head in Oregon City on or about October 17, 1850.

A tale of two Indians

In order to apprehend the history of Seattle, you have to get into the Indian political situation at the time the Americans began to trickle into the area north of the Columbia River . . . and to acquire an appreciation of the toughest Indian chief in the Puget Sound Basin.

All of our history books, for instance, cite Chief Seattle as one of Nature's noblemen . . . a chief of great oratorical abilities and of stature among the other Indians on the Sound . . . when the truth is that he was kind of a big, bumbling idiot who couldn't punch his way out of a cedar bark bag. It was a condition that went double for the other braves in his tribe—or he would never have made it as chief. He was a guy who knew how to play his politics well and could pit various factions against each other. He didn't invent the system, but he knew how to work it. The most important thing he did in his life was butter up Doc Maynard. That's why the town was named for him. But when you think of Chief Seattle, think of Charlie McCarthy on Edgar Bergen's knee. The words came out of Seattle's mouth and you couldn't even see Doc Maynard's lips moving.

The tough Indian on the Sound was Chief Patkanim.

An early history pointed out that Patkanim was "a man of bright, intelligent face, which was broad and full, eyes large and lustrous, set straight in his head, a straight Greek nose, delicate mouth with thin lips and graceful curve at the corners and the 'Cupid's bow.' He was ambitious and knew how to gain ascendancy over others . . . he was shrewd, ruthless, cunning."

Today he could be, say, a vice president of Boeing . . . maybe even president.

Patkanim was chief of the Snoqualmie and/or Snohomish tribe, the biggest and most powerful tribe on the Sound.

The tribes were named for the rivers on which they operated. So Patkanim controlled the rivers to the main passes through the Cascade Mountains (known today as Stevens and Snoqualmie). His headquarters probably was at the spot where the Snoqualmie and Skykomish rivers join to form the Snohomish—or in the neighborhood of Everett.

Chief Seattle held sway over a loose amalgamation of tribes at the mouth of the Duwamish River, which was created by the Black (no longer in existence), the Green and the White. In order to understand the situation, you must know of another chief called "Old Graybeard," who headed up a bunch of Indians near the mouth of the Nisqually River, which lies between Tacoma and Olympia.

In 1848 Chief Patkanim called together a meeting of all of the Puget Sound Indians—of which there were about 8,000—on Whidbey Island, where he pointed out that the "white" situation was getting out of hand and what the Indians should do was kill them all off before they took over the whole Puget Sound region.

Old Graybeard got up and said something like, "Yeah, and if we kill them all off, who will there be to protect my tribe against your periodic raids?" It took all the guts he had to say that.

Chief Seattle proved even more foolish.

He got up and said that his tribe occupied the land between Patkanim and Old Graybeard and he would protect the Nisquallies.

When the general hilarity among the Indians present had subsided,

Graybeard announced he'd rather have "one Boston (American) with one gun protecting us than all of the Duwamish Indians put together."

And Chief Seattle's tit really was in a ringer.

His favorite stamping ground at the mouth of the Duwamish no longer was available to him because it would be too easy for Patkanim to swoop down on him, killing warriors and taking women and children as slaves . . . which was why Chief Seattle and his tribe happened to be wintering in Olympia a couple of years later when Doc Maynard came along.

Patkanim hit the white history books again in 1849 when most of the white population on Puget Sound had departed for the California gold rush.

What he did at this time was stage a raid on the Hudson's Bay Company trading post at Fort Nisqually.

How he did it is the tricky part.

Patkanim went inside the fort, pretending he wanted to register a complaint about Graybeard and Company with factor William Tolmie. While he was there, he "accidentally" discharged his gun. His warriors attacked. Somebody providently closed the gates, but in the meantime two white men were killed.

Patkanim, who had arranged the whole show, could and did disclaim all responsibility for the attack and could get away with it because he was inside the fort at the time it occurred.

By that time the United States had taken over the territory and decided to make a *cause celebre* of the case . . . showing the Indians they couldn't get away with this kind of thing and demonstrating the American Judicial System in action. What Governor Joseph Lane did was move an entire court, including judge, jury and lawyers, up from Salem and stage a big show. The problem they encountered was finding some defendants until Chief Patkanim announced that for a hefty fee, he would produce the culprits.

Chief Patkanim delivered his own brother to be hung.

Thirty pieces of silver?

Hell, no!

Of the $2,000 it cost to stage this show, Patkanim got five hundred bucks.

The sixty-two-cent battleship

Well, it wasn't exactly a battleship.

It was an Indian war canoe. But these were substantial vessels constructed by hollowing out cedar logs, the like of which you can't even imagine today. There was a cedar tree in Doc Maynard's claim with a root system covering an entire city block. And the Indians were so adept at handling cedar that you wouldn't believe that, either.

Of course the Indians didn't work as hard as we do at the same things we do. All they had to do was work a couple of weeks in the fall during the salmon runs.

That gave 'em time to make cedar planks and use the bark of the cedar to make their clothing. And, cutting down a cedar tree with a diameter of twelve or fifteen feet with a stone ax took a little doing.

Hollowing it out into a craft twenty or thirty feet long was another time consumer.

The resulting craft was a thing of beauty with long, tapering lines that raised to a height of maybe six feet at the bow like the prow of a Viking ship. It would hold a dozen or more warriors—or an entire family with all its goods. With a sail in the bow, Indians used them to hunt whales way to hell and gone out in the Pacific. Behind the sail was a tent big enough to keep everybody covered as they sailed along in the rain, pretty as you please.

Patkanim had the best war canoe on Puget Sound.

What he did was take newly arrived white men on trips around the Sound—sort of like Western Tours or Gray Line does today.

Only, Western Tours and Gray Line bring 'em back.

One of the confrontations between the whites and Patkanim came when he took the new engineer for a sawmill on a trip around the

Sound. The engineer didn't come back. But a couple of Patkanim's braves came back wearing his clothes and carrying his watch and wallet. This was a source of considerable agitation among the other newly arrived whites in Seattle.

Patkanim allayed their fears.

He had both of his men hung . . .

Not for being thieves, but for getting caught.

And so it was on November 18, 1850, that Doc Maynard returned to Olympia, checked Catherine's Guilt Complex Temperature, found it still rising . . . and noted in his diary that he was taking a trip "down Sound."

With Patkanim, and a dozen or so of his braves.

The doctor would be gone for the next forty-five days.

But the item of interest here he entered in his diary a week after he started. He notes that he paid for one Indian canoe "one blanket, two shirts, three looking glasses and other iktas . . .

"To the amount of *sixty-two cents!*"

That made the doctor the proud new owner of Patkanim's prized Indian War Canoe . . .

Sixty-two cents.

You couldn't buy one today for $10,000.

Some deal!

How did a gentle pacifist like Doc Maynard do it? Simple. On the night of November 17, he refrained from eating dinner . . . For a simple reason.

He had dumped a dollop of ipecac in the stew.

It wrenched his heart to see those wretched red wretches reeling and retching in the rain—but it was either him or them and he knew it. And while they were engaged in this serious physical exercise he calmly informed them that, unlike other white people in the Pacific Northwest, he was not out to kill them.

On the other hand, if they so much as touched a hair on his head, this is how they would feel for the rest of their lives. He also thought it was a good time to make a deal on his future transportation needs in the new country where all transportation was by water.

If the doctor was going to make house calls, a canoe would have to be his carriage.

From the doctor's standpoint, the "patients" treated with ipecac underwent a complete "cure." From then on—and for the rest of his life—Patkanim couldn't find poles long enough to touch the doctor with. The rest of the trip around the Sound was "on the house." And from then until he died of natural causes in 1859, Patkanim wouldn't make a momentous decision like going to the bathroom without consulting Doc. I must confess the idea was not original with Doc Maynard. He'd picked it up from Dr. Marcus Whitman who had "doctored" a couple of melons with ipecac to keep the Indians out of his watermelon patch in Walla Walla.

A site for sore eyes

Doc Maynard's diary shows that they left camp early on November 19 and made it twenty miles to what we now know as the Tacoma Narrows. On the twentieth, running before a southwest wind, they made it into Commencement Bay where he bought salmon, potatoes and a new tent cover for the canoe from some Indians. This is the site of Tacoma today.

He got a lesson in Puget Sound tides that night.

I wouldn't want to say this is what soured him on Tacoma—a tradition maintained by Seattleites to this day—but he notes that he and the others "camped on the beach, but were driven off before daylight by the tide . . ."

They didn't have tide tables in those days and the tides around the Sound were unpredictable enough that even the Indians got caught short by them once in a while. There must have been some scrambling in the dark, rain and wind of that November night.

But all he notes in his diary is "Got my gun wet. Left the skillet cover."

The next day they picked up what he described as a "stiff breeze and ran around to an Indian camp where we were obliged to stay until the next morning . . ."

This was an empty Indian camp at the mouth of the Duwamish River.

Left empty by virtue of the fact that Chief Seattle and his braves were skulking around the streets of Olympia under the aegis of the white men who protected them against the dreaded Patkanim.

It was the doctor's first look at the site where he later would build the city of Seattle.

Doc Maynard, naturally, didn't describe it.

But he knew all about it from the clipping he had picked up in Oregon City the month before. Ebey noted that the Duwamish River dropped into a "bay which forms a beautiful little harbor about four miles in width and some six miles in length." He also pointed out that the river descended from a fertile valley and had an average width of about "forty yards with a deep channel and placid current." He added that "other plains of more extensive character are represented as being near at hand, and of sufficient fertility to satisfy the most fastidious taste."

It should be noted here that Ebey was more interested in farm land than in a city site. However, he described Lake Washington, which he called Lake Geneva, and adds that, "Between the lake and Admiralty Inlet (Puget Sound) the distance to Geneva Lake (which today is the narrow waist of the Queen City along Yesler Way) in many places cannot exceed a few miles as the Indians make portage across it with their canoes . . ."

The doctor had found the site of Cleveland West.

It didn't click with him at the time because he knew from Patkanim that the Duwamish River did not come down out of the mountains from the lowest pass. The pass from which this river descended (Naches) was not traversible in the winter. Patkanim, Chief of the Snoqualmie and Snohomish tribes, was proud of the fact that his tribe occupied the mouth of the two rivers which provided access to the lowest pass (Snoqualmie) and was eager to get the doctor to his own camping ground.

The doctor's principal objective was finding a good bed of coal. Everybody "knew" there would be plenty of iron ore some place in the Cascade Mountains. But the development of that resource would take time.

The urgent necessity to the doctor was coal.

The role of coal

Those of you who have read *Sons of the Profits* will have discovered, as I did, how important coal was as a resource in King County and how the forthright "sons" got squabbling among themselves and blew away the most important asset the county had—even more important than the timber or fish resources.

What additional research on the part of others and myself has brought to light during the intervening years is the importance with which Doc Maynard regarded this commodity while he still was in charge of the whole operation on Elliott Bay.

Patkanim, of course, was pretty eager to let the man with the magic in the black bag know how important Snoqualmie Pass was.It was the principal "grease trail" in the trade between the Puget Sound and Eastern Washington Indians. It was over this "trail" that the oil from the Eulachon—otherwise known as candlefish—was carried. It was this oil that was used to light the lamps of the wigwams in Eastern Washington. The Indians on the other side of the mountains could get their own salmon when that animal reached the heads of the streams. But the Eulachon oil was a different proposition. Patkanim's key position at the mouth of the important Snohomish made him the richest and most powerful chief on the Sound.

But the doctor was interested in coal.

At the time he came west, the entire nation was talking about railroads . . . more specifically, the transcontinental railroads . . . and even more specifically than that, which of the three potential trans-

continentals would be the most important: the one that would terminate in San Diego . . . the one in San Francisco or the one that
would terminate either at the mouth of the Columbia or somewhere
near the Strait of Juan de Fuca.

As soon as the doctor had settled in his mind that his future lay in the
Pacific Northwest, he became a proponent of the Puget Sound route
for the major transcontinental railroad. It was his conviction that some
town on Puget Sound would become the greatest maritime center on
the Pacific Coast. There was talk, for instance, of how fast a person
could be transported across the country.

He had just completed a trip of five months.

Railroad experts estimated that it could be done in five days!

One expert put it like this: "The eastern portions of Asia, including
China and Japan, and countries adjacent, which are known to contain
a population of many millions, in an advanced stage of civilization, in
a condition to furnish a very profitable commerce; a commerce which
has greatly enriched all that have hitherto participated in it, are
situated from three to seven thousand miles from our Pacific Coast."

The big population centers were the cities of Canton, Nanking and
Peking in China and Tokyo in Japan . . . each containing populations
of from one to two million inhabitants . . . and each having ports
accessible to U.S. vessels.

From New York to the Yangtze River, the shortest and most direct line
was over the Great Circle which runs considerably north of the
boundary between the United States and Canada. But the Strait of
Juan de Fuca provided access to U.S. harbors closest to the true curve
of the earth. The city of Chicago was the largest western city close to
the Great Circle and the natural route for the railroad ran through
Chicago via Lake Superior. The route then would go up the great
bend of the Missouri River and over one of several passes in the
Rockies located by Lewis and Clark and then down the other side
along the Columbia.

The route then would abort the valley of the Columbia, somewhere in
what we know today as Eastern Washington and cross the Cascade

Range for a more direct shot at the Strait of Juan de Fuca than could be had from the mouth of the Columbia.

The distance from Chicago to the Strait of Juan de Fuca by doing this was 1,960 miles . . .

By far the shortest route from Chicago to the Pacific Coast.

Everybody in the nation at that point knew about Mount Rainier from elevations taken by Wilkes nine years earlier. Surveyors had Mount Rainier at an elevation of 12,330 feet at the time (the official elevation is now 14,408) and figured that mountains on either side in the Cascade Range became progressively lower.

One expert made the estimate that somewhere north of Rainier a pass of 4,000 feet or less would be discovered within the next few years. And this, because it would be the closest to the Strait, would become the most important pass on the transcontinental railroad route.

A further argument for the northern route lay in three things: There were vast mineral resources, especially coal which would be the basic source of energy for the steam engines . . . timber along the entire route that was readily available to be made into ties . . . and that as fast as the line was built, the land around it would be settled by immigrants.

Bituminous coal had been discovered between Mandan and Great Falls along the Missouri.

A New York magazine of general circulation summarized the kind of thing that Doc Maynard was looking for in his first exploration of Puget Sound:

"West of the Cascade Mountains, bituminous coal is now known to exist in large quantities in the vicinity of the waters of the Straits of de Fuca . . . It lies near the surface, is gotten out with crowbars, is near to good anchorage and is of excellent quality, running in extensive folds, and even in clumpy mounds . . . most easily worked all along this part of the country."

At the time the doctor was doing his explorations, no coal had been found south of the Stillaguamish River.

The doctor didn't find the "easy access" supply of coal on that trip.

But nowhere did he find a better harbor than the one he had seen in Elliott Bay his third night out. The Indians told him that Isaac Ebey had preceded him in his explorations.

He decided to visit Ebey and talk things over.

Patkanim had no problem finding the place.

It was the exact spot where he'd called the big conclave of Indians.

The same place where Chief Seattle lost his figurative shirt.

"Colonel Ebey, I presume?"

Isaac Neff Ebey always has had a big ride in Washington history, primarily on account of the fact that the Haida Indians cut off his head and took it north with them, keeping it for two years until it was recovered by Hudson's Bay Company detectives and returned to his widow.

But, outside of the archives, nothing ever had been printed about the critically important meeting between him and Doctor Maynard in the winter of 1850.

Ebey, another Ohioan, was eight years Doc Maynard's junior and had been educated as a lawyer, but never been admitted to the bar. In 1843, he married and two sons were the result of that union. In 1846, when the younger son was but six months old, Ebey came west seeking a permanent home for his family . . .

And didn't see his wife for the next four years.

He filed his donation claim on a beautiful piece of rolling prairie land on Whidbey Island on October 15, 1850, and was living alone in his cabin there in December when Patkanim brought Doc Maynard to the spot . . . and the two men became fast friends. Both of them well educated and with a broad view of the potential of the Pacific Northwest, they had a great deal in common. They were a discouraged pair at the time. Ebey was lonesome for his wife. And the doctor didn't know whether it was up, down or sideways with Catherine.

The doctor had been led to believe in everything he had read that there were enormous coal deposits somewhere around the Canadian border . . . but none of his explorations had turned up anything worthwhile. It has to be presumed that Ebey, who was enthusiastic about the site of what became King County, persuaded the doctor that this was the spot where coal would be found and where the major city of the Pacific Northwest would grow.

The doctor, in turn. learned that Ebey had political ambitions, and filed away this knowledge for future use.

Ebey later would file an affidavit with the Oregon Territorial Legislature that : "This is to certify that I have been acquainted with the bearer, D. S. Maynard, since some time in the autumn of 1850 and am happy in saying that I consider him a man of honest moral principles and believe that he is considered as such among his acquaintances in general."

Doc Maynard returned to Olympia toward the end of December, realizing that what he was, was broke.

Doc Maynard's incredible woodpile

The way Prosch put it was: "Urgent necessity stared him boldly and harshly in the face. Undaunted, he took off his fine coat, donned the garments of a laborer, and proceeded to cut cordwood for the San Francisco market." Being the kind of man he was, however, it couldn't be just any old woodpile.

It had to be the biggest pile of wood on earth.

There also had to be an angle or two that didn't meet the naked eye.

If anything ever was prime example of the inventor of Seattle in action, the pile of wood that he cut in Olympia between January and August, 1851, is it . . . because, of course, he had another ax to grind than the one he was using to cut down those trees and then split them up into four-foot sections of cordwood for the San Francisco market. All he has ever gotten in our official history books on this one is a couple of lines in a footnote or two saying that he, personally, cut 400 cords of wood in a period of eight months.

However, for 125 years, historians have agreed that he did cut them and he did cut them all by himself. He interrupted his woodcutting from time to time to take an interest in the future state of Washington and to thwart the mighty Mike Simmons, which he could be persuaded to do as easy as you could spit in the street . . .

Easier.

And to pursue the hand of the beautiful maiden that Mike kept locked up in the castle on the other side of the moat.

Well, it really wasn't much of a moat.

It was Mike's combined house, store and post office at First and Main Street in Olympia . . . although during the rainy winter months, both First and Main were muddy enough to satisfy the qualifications of a moat, which the dictionary describes as a "deep and wide trench around a fortified place, usually filled with water."

Take a look at "General" Maynard's strategy.

In those days a man could keep all the wood he could cut. And the place he chose to do his cutting was on the outskirts of Olympia along Budd Inlet, where every passing ship could see the results of his work.

Every night he could tramp into town and sit someplace jawing with the boys and keep an eye out for Catherine. Mike couldn't keep a guard on Catherine all of the time. And the second mighty Mike turned his back, the two lovers were in one another's arms making the most of their limited opportunities.

There also was a subtle psychological battle going on between the doctor and the merchant prince of Olympia. The folks around and about admired a man with guts. The doctor was a nobody. Mike was the man who had broken the lock the British had kept on the land north of the Columbia River. For thirty years it had been the policy of Great Britain to divert emigrants to that part of the Oregon Territory south of the Columbia River.

Great Britain figured she would have to reach a compromise with America over this ground . . . she hoped the border would follow the westward flow of the Columbia.

Mike was the first to defy Dr. John McLoughlin, chief factor of the

Hudson's Bay Company, and move north of the Columbia to settle on Puget Sound with the first American hydraulically operated saw and grist mills.

He was the most important man on the Sound.

Men didn't cross him lightly. He ran things with a strong hand. They might resent him, but they didn't cross him. And here was this mild-mannered and genial doctor, quietly and thoroughly driving Mike nuts.

It must be remembered that this was an extremely physical society. There was no electricity. There was no steam power . . . with the exception of the *Beaver,* ships that entered Puget Sound were sailing ships. Olympia was the only town on the Sound. Mike Simmons was the only merchant in the town. He had a monopoly which might make him unpopular on some fronts, but which, it was generally believed, would soon make him a millionaire.

In order to understand this, you have to understand one of the peculiarities of existence in the Pacific Northwest at that time and place.

For two or three decades the Hudson's Bay Company had, to all practical purposes, owned and operated the vast Oregon Territory.

And the company had done it through its merchandising policy. It charged reasonable prices, but it did not permit anybody else to enter the merchandising business in opposition.The company wasn't about to let somebody else enter the fur trade by importing goods to swap with the Indians for fur. As someone put it, "If you wanted to buy a new pair of trousers, you had to show the clerk the rent in the ones you were wearing before he would sell you the new ones."

When the United States got the Oregon Territory at what is generally the same boundary as today, merchants began opposing the Bay Company south of the Columbia, and because of the competition, prices were reasonable.

But Mike was the only *American* merchant on Puget Sound.

Where brooms sold for twenty-five cents in Portland and Oregon City, Mike was selling them for a dollar. Mike got a dollar a yard for calico and a dollar a pound for sugar—items that sold for two-bits south of the river. For a stove that sold for $7.50 in New York . . . $15 in San Francisco and $22.50 in Portland or Oregon City, Mike got a whopping $80.

They might not like it . . .

But if they wanted a stove, they paid it.

And here was this little old man (Doc was forty-three) with his crosscut saw and his ax and his wedges felling trees that were as high as a twenty-story building and ten or fifteen feet in diameter and splitting them into four-foot lengths and piling them into a stack that stretched along the beach north of town.

The people, with some degree of experience with doctors, were suspicious of medical men, but a man who was out there all day long, six days a week, cutting wood . . .

He was somebody they could understand.

Doc defied "Authority."

And they loved him for it.

It wasn't so much the amount of wood he cut. He only did about two cords a day and there were men in town who could cut six cords a day. It was his cheerful disposition and his persistence. He kept at that wood pile for eight months . . . steadily knocking off his two cords a day . . . and the bigger the woodpile got, the madder Mike got . . .

And the more thoughtful Catherine got.

This was really some pile of wood.

If somebody were to do it today, it would look like the wall of China in downtown Seattle.

Piled to a height of six feet, it would stretch from today's City Hall in Seattle five blocks along Fourth Avenue to the Olympic Hotel. How many men would—or even could—cut that much wood without help and without a chain saw . . . beginning with huge trees . . . in eight months time?

For a woman . . .

The "Sidney Ducks," and other wild birds

In the traditional Seattle history books, the settlers arrived here dead broke and were able to sell piling to Captain Daniel S. Howard of the brig *Leonesa* for eight cents a running foot and cordwood for four dollars a cord. They put their backs to the task and pretty soon the original economy of the city was established. The folks quickly ran out of trees at Alki Point and started cutting at places like Gig Harbor . . . and, finally staked their claims across the bay where the city is today, because here the timber was thick and easily rolled down a steep hill to deep water.

The way the usual story goes is that Captain Howard appeared with money to buy piling for the San Francisco market as if "sent by a wise Providence." They knelt and thanked God.

It wasn't a wise Providence Doc Maynard thanked . . .

It was the "Sidney Ducks" and other wild birds who populated the rougher part of San Francisco at the time. The Sidney Ducks were a gang of convicts who had escaped from Sidney, Australia, and other men of their ilk who formed gangs like the "Hounds" and the "Regulators."

Thanks to the discovery of gold, San Francisco was a boom town in the early 1850s. As *Encyclopedia Americana* puts it: "The Argonauts appeared in such great numbers that supplies and services of every sort were quickly exhausted . . . Shiploads of merchandise were brought ashore and dumped on the beach for lack of storage. Buildings about the plaza were turned into gambling resorts and brought huge profits to their operators. Because everything was in short supply, prices rose to fantastic heights. Hundreds of buildings of canvas or wood were hastily erected to house stores, banks or offices, and when these were swept away in the frequent fires they were promptly rebuilt . . ."

All of which brings us to the gangs.

For a while these fellas just rolled drunks for their money, which was kind of a piecemeal, retail operation.

The big money lay in looting.

Well, murder offered an enterprising young man some incentive, but it was hard to tell in advance whether there were any real bucks in it.

But loot . . . that was a sure thing.

These entrepreneurs quickly realized that for any kind of a healthy economy in the looting business, it was necessary to have something to loot. And the best insurance for that was a fire. By the very nature of things, what with the population of San Francisco growing from 800 to 35,000 in a couple of years, fires were an enormous hazard. With the aid of the Barbary Coast gangs, they became a routine method of doing business.

Between 1849 and 1851 the town was burned down five times.

So, while the early settlers on Elliott Bay blessed The Lord for providing them with a solution to their economic problems, it really was The Devil.

The beneficent Captain Howard provided those original settlers at Alki Point with eight cents a running foot for pilings which he sold in San Francisco for a dollar a running foot.

Doc had plenty of opportunities to sell his woodpile for four bucks a cord, but he had a different proposition in mind. He didn't want a buyer. He wanted a partner. And finally, in the fall of 1851, he found the right man in Captain L. M. Felker of the brig *Franklin Adams.* Felker at first agreed to charter his boat to Maynard. The cordwood was excellent collateral. He would be paid when it sold in San Francisco. Felker so admired the doctor's persuasiveness that he subsequently went into partnership with him.

Doc accompanied his pile of wood to California and sold that 400 cords of wood in San Francisco for forty dollars a cord . . . *sixteen thousand bucks!* (The equivalent of $155,000 in today's money.)

That was the $16,000 which financed the invention of Seattle.

All's Weller that ends Weller

One of those quickie historians who zips around the world doing instant analyses of cities had kind of a lucky strike a number of years ago when he compared San Francisco to a man's mistress and Seattle to a man's wife. And without getting into the question of whether mistresses are more interesting people than wives, this small observation is a reflection of one facet of Doc Maynard's personality.

He was the first one to toss the pebble in the still lake of the virgin territory, and the waves he made have been making a widening circle ever since.

His association with John Weller is a case in point.

Weller performed a great service to the doctor when the latter was deeply distressed at home. He got the doctor out of the house and into politics, and if he had won the gubernatorial campaign, Doc might have gone to Columbus instead of Oregon. Weller, who had four wives and thought the doctor was out of his mind to attach that much importance to any one woman, was the catalyst who got the doctor away from Cleveland . . . although Maynard wasn't *going* anywhere.

He was a fugitive *from* somewhere.

It was a part and parcel of the doctor's character, however, that he felt some kind of moral obligation to Weller . . . so when Maynard arrived in San Francisco and sold his firewood, he took the time to trundle over to the goldfields and what turned out to be his final meeting in Sacramento with his old friend.

In a classic sense, Weller offered the ultimate bribe. He pointed to a chest of gold in his tent and told the doctor he could keep all that he could carry away. The powerfully built doctor who just had completed eight months of hard labor in the woods had a fortune at his fingertips.

When Maynard smiled and declined the offer, Weller knew that their close association was a thing of the past, and, like any good politician, accepted the decision with grace; and the conversation drifted into other channels. But the life in California was distasteful to Doc. While he was in Sacramento, five men were killed in one nearby camp and several others killed in the neighborhood. At the time he was in San Francisco, the town established some kind of a record with 1,000 murders a year.

Weller suggested that Maynard get into the lumber business. In those days you could buy all of the machinery necessary for a sawmill for $15,000. "Give up your profession," Weller said. "Get the machinery for a sawmill. In selling us lumber you'll make a hundred dollars for every one you may possibly make in doctoring and you'll soon be rich."

But the doctor wasn't interested in making small pieces of wood out of big ones.

He'd got a bellyfull of that in the past eight months.

And the wheels within the wheels of Fate were meshing for him even in his visit to California. Weller informed him that a couple of fellow Ohioans, John Stroble and Henry Yesler, had purchased the machinery necessary for a steam sawmill. Weller had heard from Yesler's wife, Sarah, who had arranged the financing. The machinery was en route to San Francisco. Mrs. Yesler had written everyone she knew—including Weller—in search of her husband. She was afraid the machinery would arrive and be sold for freight charges. And Yesler was missing.

When last heard from, the two men had investigated Marysville,

California, for a mill site and were headed to the Pacific Northwest. Weller suggested that the doctor might want the mill in the town he was proposing to build on Puget Sound.

The doctor was well aware of the importance of having the first steam sawmill on Puget Sound in his town. Most existing Seattle histories hold that Yesler talked Maynard out of the land for his sawmill.

The truth is the exact opposite.

The land was waiting for Yesler before the doctor ever met him or Yesler ever put in an appearance on Puget Sound.

Weller's final contribution to the construction of Seattle fell into place when he introduced the doctor to one George N. McConaha, another Ohioan. McConaha, like Maynard, had been summoned by Weller when the latter decided he wanted to become the first United States senator when California became a state. And McConaha had performed well on Weller's behalf. As a member of California's first state legislature, he had lobbied through Weller's nomination and appointment to the Senate by that body.

At the time the doctor was in Sacramento, McConaha was serving as the prosecuting attorney for the city of Sacramento.

Within six months, he would be at Doc Maynard's doorstep.

Out of loyalty, friendship or whimsy, Doc Maynard named one of the streets in his original plat of Seattle after his friend, Weller. Today, the bottom of that street originates in one of the facilities in the Kingdome Stadium . . .

And the least we could do is name it the "John Weller Memorial Men's Room."

Doctor, Lawyer, Merchant Chief

Things were clicking into place with uncanny precision while Maynard was in California.

When he returned to San Francisco from Sacramento, it was to find Captain Felker waiting for him along with what today would be called the world's biggest garage sale. There were more than 500 ships laying abandoned in San Francisco Bay as a result of the fact that the crews left them for the gold fields as soon as they hit dry land. A lot of them still had their cargoes on board.

And, for pennies on the dollar, the doctor purchased enough merchandise to load Felker's brig to the gunwales. When they started north, the doctor had enough in the way of goods to start two or three general stores . . . and he was only out five hundred bucks.

In those days, the going rate for starting a town was $3,000 . . . What you could buy for the three thousand was a fishery, a barrel factory, the necessary equipment for cutting piling and shingles and for hewing timbers. It also included the necessities for opening a general store.

Felker figured the doctor was some kind of a genius.

Maynard had enough capital to start *five* towns!

Felker went into partnership with the doctor.

And an excellent plan it was. The doctor could produce the cargoes for San Francisco on Puget Sound. Felker could provide merchandise for the store in the Bay City . . . and they could split the profits on both. Felker's role in the founding of Seattle always has been passed over as amounting to very little when the truth is that his was a key position from the beginning.

As the saying goes, "when you're hot, you're hot . . ." And, as the two partners made the turn into the Strait of Juan de Fuca at Cape Flattery, the Makah Indians were about to dispose of the contents of a wrecked ship along with the passengers and crew.

Felker had a little brass cannon on the bow of the *Franklin Adams*. A few well placed shots dispersed the Indians and saved the people and the ship's cargo. The people were Canadians. Felker and the doctor took them and their possessions to Victoria where the authorities rewarded them with enough cash and goods to start yet another town.

Doc Maynard kept the little brass cannon as a souvenir . . . and during his lifetime—perhaps even longer—it was fired on the Fourth of July and other civic occasions.